# GARDEN RAIL
## FROM THE GROUND UP

*IOW County Press*

# David Pratt

# GARDEN RAILWAYS
## FROM THE GROUND UP

## David Pratt

Published by David Pratt

First published 2006. Copyright David Pratt
Printing services, Biltmore Printers, Newport IOW
Author, and illustrations except where credited, David Pratt
Design and layout: David Pratt
ISBN:      0-9552598-0-0
(978-0-9552598-0-7)

# Acknowledgements

The genesis for this book was a telephone call from sound recordist Mark Found. He knew that I built railways, and his uncle Dikram had left him a mountain of LGB model items, including enough track to reach the moon it seemed. Discovery Television channel were persuaded to fund a series. Positive Productions came to me for my advice and to appear as consultant. Mark assumed the role of presenter. I saw that a book was needed, so did Michael Adamson at GRS.

It's called 'Vanity Publishing' but, unlike Lazlo Biro, Mr. Walschaert, or the Earl of Sandwich, becoming famous isn't my motivation. My wish is simply to draw attention to our hobby, and correct the belief that it has to be expensive to run trains in the garden, and you have to be a hundred years old – with a grey beard.

A thank you to Brian Cantwell, for the covers, Laurence Nott of LearnDirect, who taught me about production, John Simes who took time away from golf (sad) to read my words. To John Goodwin, who cleaned my carpets the other day. He was a fireman at 'Top Shed' Kings Cross. He actually fired Mallard.

*A note to me from Alan Titchmarsh, July 2005…..*
"Alan admits he has only ever seen one or two miniature railways in gardens, and probably never on television…..and if it were to encourage children out into the garden, he'd be even more keen (he has his own charity, *gardens for schools)*".

# Index

# 1. Welcome to our hobby

*Railway enthusiasm affects the young as well as the old. Everyone that you know will have seen Thomas the Tank Engine or Hogwarts express. The excitement of a train journey enhanced by some understanding of the professional skills of railwaymen. These are motivations for recreating something of railways in miniature.*

Why in our gardens? Our gardens are now an extension of our homes, a room outside, for relaxation and play.

FAQs? Frequently asked questions. I started my garden railway involvement after impulse buying a huge green loco like I had only seen as a boy in Bassett-Lowke's shop window. This turned out to be an LGB 'Stainz' with sound in the cab. Next, though I had no railway, a Lionel 4-4-2 G-Scale American loco, and an aluminium passenger car. My mantlepiece was now full. I had to start on the railway.

**G-Scale LGB runs behind decorative wall round a corner. Pillars are drainpipes on end, supporting sleepers.**

For many, the decisions are. Where do I start? What scale? What gauge can I use? What kind of railway will I model – mainline, or narrow gauge? Where in the world? Electric power, or live steam? What era?

Like any new hobby or interest, a little research is useful. There is only one magazine available to us in the U.K. and back issues are cheaper. A handful of Garden Rail magazines will give an overview and show the main players making and selling equipment. Recently there was only one book – my previous one.

**The television series 'The Garden Railway' available on DVD, shows a small garden railway being built from scratch – which took three weeks in reality.**

The next most useful document is the big Garden Railway Specialists catalogue. This lists almost everything that you will need, and there are many detailing accessories for later. Some or all of the above should set you on the right road to pre-planning a railway in your garden. Membership of a club or society will provide useful local inspection visits.

## Scales are for Fish!

***The best museum exhibits, like the best dioramas, vary the scale of objects with distance. Larger near the viewer, and smaller as the distance increases.***

We can increase the apparent depth/distance by this means in our garden railways. After all, the real plants are not to scale, we simply chose smaller leafed plants near the railway. The clever part is to vary size as we go away from the railway till we can safely have regular sized plants in our view. This all maintains the illusion of our world in miniature.

**A real mixture of scales that work together in the garden. G-1 to G-Scale figures, G3 loco, B.O.B. buildings and even a twelfth scale doll's house garden bottom left.**

The station photograph is composed of several scale elements, which work together. The station building suits Gauge –1 and G-Scale. Evergreen station from B.O.B. has mixed Gauge-1 and G-Scale figures on its platform, The GWR Pannier tank is Gauge-3 (G-Scale but wider tracks), the visible part of the track is 64mm 'standard gauge', and the modelled garden is doll's house one twelfth scale. I have used various resin cast gardens, even plastic grass, in garden railways.

Many of us forget that although we can model exact scaled down bricks (9"x41/2"x3") how big is the building made with them? Guilford Cathedral is made of bricks. Bricks used to be laid to 'imperial' measure, now the same bricks are laid in 'metric' measure. This just means (a lot) more mortar in between.

*We still buy four inch nails by the kilo! In our outdoor garden railway world, we can sometimes be too preoccupied with scale.*

GAUGE

A great many of us run LGB, on 45mm gauge track. The mainstay of their (1:22.5) G-Scale models were Swiss, German and Austrian *narrow gauge* railways. These were a mixture of two foot and metre gauges. However, LGB also model American 'wild west' trains, which ran on *standard gauge* 4ft 81/2inch track. Recently, several more LGB standard gauge models appeared – the LCE express runs on standard gauge tracks through modern Germany. On the same LGB G-Scale 45mm rails this *must* mean that the model is Gauge-1? Their U.S. Alco FA1 diesels and aluminium coaches – *standard gauge* trains. Their magnificent SNCF pacific loco – again *standard gauge*, pulling the shortened Orient Express coaches (sort of G-Scale), so this train must be Gauge-1 as well! Like I said, scales are for fish?

SCALE

We also use (Faller) marked 'Pola-G' plastic buildings. Some of the kits even have Pola-LGB embossed on them, and some of the boxes show 1:22.5 (G-Scale) as the scale. However, if we put a number of buildings in close proximity and look at the doors – the only obvious scale indicator, we can see Gauge-1 through to 16mmNG (1:19) will be served. One or two models, such as the 'small smithy' which gives its original dimensions, is possibly even right for (1:43) Gauge 'O'!

British Outline Buildings are designed for all the garden 'scenic scales'. The doors are cleverly designed to set models to particular scales simply by the way they are painted. The modelled nine-inch bricks are 12mm long equalling 16mm (1:19) to the foot, but some buildings are small, some large – and it works!

**Main Line? Express? Gauge-1 Aster A4 live steam and Gresley teak coaches.**

To add to the appreciation of scale, In my photo above, of B.O.B. buildings station scene, the G-Scale porter (Preiser G) seems to have asked for his weeks pay in cash – that's a fifty pence piece he's having trouble with. My first wages as a junior on British Rail Western Region in 1960 were - twelve shillings and sixpence a week. A little over 50p. So you see, it's all relative really.

**Modelling a prototype from real life. Glyn Valley Tramway, though long gone, has a large 16mm (1:19) following. This kit is by B.O.B. from J.A.Replicas.**

Now what about gauge? Did you buy a starter set, or a loco, like me, and follow on in G-Scale 45mm gauge Usually these models are 1:22.5 (13.5mm/ft) but even the initiators of this scale, LGB, have taken liberties. Other manufacturers produce 1:20.3, 1:24, 1:29 and sometimes 1:30 scale 'G-Scale' models. However, these all run on the same gauge tracks with the rails set 45mm apart.

We mustn't forget the gardening aspect of our hobby. A well integrated railway satisfies the railwayman, and the gardener. Not always the same person, and an opportunity to interest others in what we do outdoors.

Recap then, LGB model European and American railways from the nineteenth century to the present day. The railways are narrow gauge 2 - 3ft6in gauges as well as 'standard' gauge, all running on LGB 45mm trackwork.
A new 'standard gauge' G-Scale, modelling mainline (4ft 81/2in) trains, running on 63.5mm spaced rails – same as the old Gauge-3, is expanding rapidly with British model rolling stock and accessories. This lends itself to a narrow gauge line alongside a 'mainline' or a junction interchange, everything is the same scale

Even before LGB came along, modellers were running 'Gauge-1' trains out of doors. Mostly manual live-steam, which necessitated tracks about 30ins above the ground so that the 'driver' could run alongside. Gauge-1 therefore is not always one of the 'scenic scales' where infrastructure modelling and planting are important. This also can apply to the long established – SM32 mostly R/C these days, narrow gauge models at 16mm/ft (1:19) running on 'O' gauge at 32mm gauge spacing.

**Loco is standard gauge G-scale. Kit is £600.**

**Resin outdoor buildings suit all the 'scenic scales'. The coal wagon and track are 'OO'**

The next question is a little harder. Will I model prototype? That is, from real and existing or now gone, railways. These were and are main line or narrow gauge, with some specialities as well. Alternatively, my railway will be made up of whatever I like – freelance. Freelance can apply to the rolling stock and locos too. Many manufacturers of live steam locos prefer to produce 'generic' engines that look the part but are not modelled on any original. There are no restrictions, I am always surprised by something new

### At a recent show I found a 'fantasy' loco reminiscent of Roland Emett and Heath Robinson. Are you having Disney spells?

The interest that we have does not have to be solely running trains. The operation, signalling, marshalling of freight, modelling a busy terminus or country junction. The electronics for automated control, perhaps with computer programming might attract youngsters away form their X-Box or Playstation and may involve others, perhaps a school project involvement.

Simple gardening, involving construction of a rockery, has inspired many to add cable cars, rack railway, or more.
There are those whose passion is gardening and are already outdoors, a new area, alpines or herbs will beckon. Children can become excited by any and every area of skill, their curiosity is boundless.

For me, the next part is the most enjoyable – planning the line. I prefer gardens that are *not* level so that there are challenges in the form of bridges and tunnels. Gradients will need special attention, or will the line be flat, whatever the lie of the land?

This also means that we can undertake long term garden restructuring, perhaps on retirement or arrival in a new home. I believe that the garden design should be paramount, with the railway integrating to this, just as real railway engineers had to solve their problems, though they didn't have to go round trees.

***Whatever the plan, and the predicted size of the railway, it helps to get something running early on.***

Sometimes, it pays to begin with a 'starter set' to get the feel and idea of its size for your garden railway.

This circle can remain as you develop the layout, as a test track for new purchases, or for the youngsters with their Playmobil trains. Even as a live steam only line or for visitors on 'old' analogue, while you move on to digital control of the newest models available.

**English garden, American Alco FA-1, G-Scale at waist height. Ideal for viewing standing or lounging.**

Everyone needs to see trains running, otherwise impetus, and then interest is lost, by you and/or the family, and the groundworks out in the garden may remain for too long looking like a building site.

Neighbours can get very twitchy seeing trenches for track bases, though only shallow, and may think there is 'development' going on without permission. If you can, tell the neighbours what you are doing. Above all, carry the family with you.

# 2. Building out of doors

**Dublo's can do it alone in the loft, but we do it with the family – in the garden.**

*For many, the garden is possibly the largest space at our disposal at home, and we use it for our leisure activities.*
*Before we launch into the wonderful world of model railways in the real world, let me define a 'Garden railway'. I find it easy to say first what it is not – it is not just a train set in the garden. We build garden railways because they are much nearer to the real thing, and in the real world.*

The smaller the scale models and tracks are, the more vulnerable they will be in the open air. There are garden railways as small as gauge '0' outside. Jack Ray's 'Crewchester' line is the subject of at least one book. They stretch right up to five inch and seven and a quarter inch gauges, though these are classed as 'miniature railways'. There is one famous garden railway, that is four feet eight and a half inches 'standard' gauge - in the grounds of Sir William McAlpine's Henley estate.

***Our small modern gardens are so easily maintained – with a Hoover once a week, and a Rachel de Thame manicure afterwards.***

Since the nineteen seventies, when G-Scale was launched, this has been the main scale for gardens. Slightly smaller, Gauge-1 possibly comes second in numbers and models available. 16mm (British narrow gauge) is probably as popular and diverse. G-Scale is dominated by its inventors LGB, who started with narrow gauge Swiss, Austrian or German preserved railways, but they have extended their range of models to include several prototype gauges and newer rolling stock. Gauge One tends to be the province of fine-scale modellers/engineers and realistic live steam – with Japanese Aster producing 'Flying Scotsman' and 'Sir Nigel Gresley' models. Marklin still produce Gauge-1 highly detailed tinplate trains, zinc plated as motorcars are, for outdoor use.

**So what if it drizzles, the trains run just as well in the wet. We all benefit from fresh air.**
**A corner of a suburban garden becomes a fascinating area for children of any age.**
**Freddie can't wait.**

I have said many times, daily almost, that we true garden railway enthusiasts follow in the footsteps of the great railway pioneers such as Brunel. Our railways may be smaller but we must still overcome natural obstacles, ponds, rocks, slopes and the weather. Local wildlife will prove a challenge, with birds pecking ballast and reflections in windows. Hedgehogs hibernate in tunnels, badgers eat signals and think that red wire in the ground is a worm – supper.

Clearly, the rolling stock, buildings, electrics, must all be weatherproof. Yes we can run trains in the rain – better for electrical pickup. Snow is welcomed – we can hook up the snowplough. There are extra hazards in colder or hotter climes for those who live there, but this does not deter them.

**You *can* do this at home. Starting in a new garden or re-landscaping?**

**It's only a small garden but you can rent great machinery.**

**A small digger goes through a garden gate and can do a week's work in a day. We were in a hurry for t.v.**

The 'ride-on' and commercial railways need to be out of doors because they need the space and have to organise the viewing or riding public. There are extra hazards in train operation here. The public deserves to be protected from danger, and insurance as well as statutory regulations come into play. Planning consent, building regulations, environmental health will need attention if a larger railway is contemplated. Planning consents mean filling in forms the size of the Sunday Telegraph, and just as intelligible.

### *Many of us have turned round and looked behind us, shocked to see the enormity of twenty years pocket money and labour building the railways in our gardens.*

Standard gauge G-Scale has been growing in popularity recently, with many new products in this modelling field. The wide sweeping curves are an outdoor must. As I write this, LGB are preparing to launch their new 'lifestyle' train sets, a starter set for those who have everything?
The wider interest of railway outdoor modellers is best served by the major scales. There are level crossings, tunnel mouths (in concrete) station buildings – even villages with churches and windmills – all in Gauge –1, G-scale, 16mm.
All these are 'working' and can be illuminated at night or have digital sounds added. A model population with railwaymen, passengers and tradesmen is available, inhabiting many countries and at all periods of railway history.

### *The open air is beneficial to us all and an advantage to younger people.*

The railways do not have to represent nostalgic scenes from a bygone and fading era. The Eurostar and Bullet Train, are both available for outdoors high-speed duty.

The mountain cable car and rack railway that operates in full size in Switzerland can be seen in model form on our rockery.

**Battery powered rotating toilet brush snow plough clears the tracks and powers the loco for some Winter action.**
**Buildings left out all year round will need more maintenance attention. These are Pola ABS plastic items.**

So long as safety is a factor in the design and construction, with no mains electricity, just low voltages (usually 20 Volts) outside, danger is non existent even for very young children. There are many toys for children, including trains and passengers that will work with our G-scale railways (visit Toys R Us). The tracks need never be idle and the youngsters can do no harm (mostly!). The whole family can find interest in our railway works.

*Those who are not so agile or able-bodied, though we might have been if we'd eaten brocolli and soya crab sticks, need have no concerns.*

A proportion of the railway construction follows normal building practice. This means that with clear plans and instructions we can use local tradesmen for electrics, track base, fence and rockery building, drainage and planting. A railway on a wall is sometimes the only way to get the tracks round a corner to leave a planting space behind. The local bricklayer will give a quote for the job. In the same way the local garden centre may well deliver and assemble the needed train storage shed. Fencing installers can assemble a track base on posts, costs are not high.

Buildings Bespoke of Hereford will construct a garden shed in the shape of a guard's van (with lookout duckets) or signal box, and have plans for a diesel cab and GWR rail car cab end. Prices start at a level with garden centre big sheds.

Owner Martin built the new signal box at Welshpool railway. What better way to

It may take a while, but gardeners have patience already. A 'view from a train' waterfall with a Playmobil whitewater canoeist attempting some rapids.
This is a simple garden feature to construct, and I believe would enhance any garden – along with the railway!

A more difficult feature here - You see, trains even go together with swimming pools – in the south of France.

contemplate the garden and railway than from the guard's van balcony?

All the activities associated with garden development around a garden railway, from electric/electronics, to horticulture, and hydraulics, should draw the whole family outdoors and into new areas of interest, and often use unexpected knowledge and skills of friends and visitors.

# 3. Planning the Railway

*Outside, the absence of any specific boundaries increases the possibilities to the point where we might not know where to put the railway.*

All railways have a 'start' and 'end' point. My own planning always starts with the essential garden shed position. This will be the 'site office' during construction, house the rolling stock, and staff, be the workshop, the night–time store, and possibly the hub of the control system. It often affects the track's basic height. The chaps at GRS say it's not essential, and I guess you could run into the conservatory or kitchen, or carry trains into the 'study. If you don't give this serious consideration at the start someone in a balaclava and baggy trousers might break into your home and steal your new LGB Stainz, and your wife – don't blame me.

For me, and I suspect most others, planning our railway is an integral part of the fun of the whole project. This is not to say that railways don't develop over time, often a lifetime. The potential problems go far beyond those encountered in smaller scales indoors. Are you a 'driver', 'signalman' with lots of shunting, or 'constructor'?
In a perfect world, the planning is best done in the Winter, Groundworks undertaken in the Autumn, and left to 'settle' for next season's building and track laying. I am either too impatient for this, or my client wants to build in November (first frosts) or March (last frosts) and "run next Easter".

Perhaps the most fundamental decision is of course exactly where the railway will be. Judicious planting might hide a circular layout. There will be some ground

disturbance, and excavated material goes to the rockery area or covers the tunnels. Trackside planting can best be done when track is being laid (in the Spring?).

In a smaller garden, the railway usually runs around the perimeter. This means that the track will have to be traversed at some point to get to the centre of the garden. At ground level, concrete crossings, paths will need to be crossed. With a raised track, 'bar flaps' (ask in the local pub) or lift – out bridges might be called for.

**You will be changing the real environment, so be sure that you do it for the better.**

A second and major consideration is the minimum radius that trains will have to travel. The choice of narrow gauge meandering lines implies lots of tight radius curves. Ready made curved track sections come in three sizes and often the first choice will be the smallest, tightest. Four feet radius for 45mm and eight feet for 63.5mm G-scale 'standard gauge tracks. Remember, set track goes where it wants, flexible and you decide.

### Golden Rule: Always use the largest radius possible.

When we are forced, or plan, small radius curves we need to be aware of the implications. There will be friction, and wear over the longer term. More maintenance. You can get a pretty good idea of where the railway is going by placing sections of rail on the ground. No need to buy a pile of track, just a selection of curves and a few straights, plus some 'Flexi' for gentle curves.

Nearly all of this is avoided of course if we don't plan a 'dog bone' dumbell shaped circular layout, handy for a central station, and opt for 'end to end' or 'out and back', up and down one side, with a return circle at the end. Even here, it is tempting to use the small radius pointwork – it's the cheapest. The railway may be limited by the terrain, the topography, please don't limit it by mean trackwork.

I have talked about the gradients, soil and trackbase, with a decision on the whole concept, an overview of the type and its rough position, and provision of a home for trains, actual detailed planning can now begin. Find a pad of squared graph paper marked with existing shrubbery and trees, and some levels, grab a long drink and settle down to some day-dreaming…….. and thinking about those ample curves.

**One manufacturer used to supply large graph paper for us to plan our railways. There are several scale rulers and templates for standard radius curves.
These all assist with our dreams and plans before we venture outside.
Picture shows my proposed waist height end of line terminus with the necessary turntable. Tracks go out and back via a loop at the far end.**

# Surveying and Groundworks
## The vital first step.

*Before we can even begin to plan our railway, we need to survey our piece of land. The railway may be Gauge One or five inch ride-on but the underlying ground and how it behaves in Winter and Summer, is very important to us. This is perhaps the first preparatory step that we must take, and one that is unique in railway modelling. We are in the real world!*

With regard to the underlying soil, gardeners will already have a good idea of the way their garden works. The damp patches, the stony areas. This knowledge will become important for future planting at the trackside. Within reason, we can import various soils, and add to existing soil, or provide new drainage.
We could plan a large rockery at the bottom of the garden only to find three feet of water there after a major downpour because we have blocked the run-off. Worse, the rockery could sink down to ground level.
In Summer, a clay base will become as hard as iron, and may well shrink by inches letting our bridge topple over. This is why house foundations must be below a clay top layer.

A survey can range from the simple to the comprehensive depending on our interest or concerns and wish to use or acquire skills. At its most simple, we need to know whether our garden is level, or falls at one end or one side, and by how much. We can do this by using a garden hose with an empty drink bottle at each end. Water will be level in both, and we can mark a fence or place a stick marked at the same height wherever we go. This will let us measure down to the ground level so that we can plot the rise and fall of the garden. Taking, say, the patio or damp course as a reference 'level'. We may chose to follow natural contours with our railway but this depends on our previous choices. Rack railways will climb 1in 4 to 1in 10 slopes, about 1in 25 limits most G-scale electric traction (LGB Railbus climbs well), 1in40 is probably a maximum for most live steamers.

There are simple viewing devices from hire shops that are levelled with a bubble, then we look around the garden through a little telescope with cross hairs, and mark as before. Perhaps the simplest of all is to use as long a spirit level as we can get, even attaching this to a long straight piece of plank wood or metal, and knock pegs into the ground along the railway area so that the tops are level. We could push canes into the soil and attach white sticky labels. Recently, spirit levels with projector lasers which shine a red dot over long distance have appeared. These allow us to fix the 'master base level' and mark its equivalent all over the garden quickly and easily. If the USAF shopped in Woolworths, friendly fire might not happen. Woolworths even sell a brilliant 'red dot' laser level for ten pounds.

**Woolworths laser level for £10.**
**A new hi-tech way to mark a level all round your garden whatever its size.**
**Track height can be measured down from these points.**
**This allows us to incorporate precise gradients or keep tracks exactly level as we wish.**
**Brunel would have wanted one.**

We do not need to mark the anticipated track level but simply make marks that are *level with each other* all over the railway area. Perhaps we can put a 'master' mark on a distant fence post so that we can refer back to it in the future. When we have several level marks, we can measure down from them to where we want the track base to be.

### We do not want our railway tracks to be level. Slopes make for more interest, and with live steam, they make the driver's experience more enjoyable.

I have grown to dislike railways on the ground. Because I have built too many in Winter. They suffer from so many problems in building and operating, us older persons do not want to spend great amounts of time on frosty ground on our knees. Frost, damp, earthworms and other wildlife will use the railway as their motorway, leaves will accumulate, weeds grow, and birds peck the ballast away.

A viewing height six feet or so above the railway is a bad viewing angle, this means we look down on the tops of buildings and trains as though in a helicopter – quite unreal. Just by raising the railway a few inches or more, we have a comfortable working height, at about two feet high, we can see the trains better from a seated position – side on, the rain can drain away, ground frosts are rarer, and the wind can blow leaves away. Sort this one out for yourself, as you plan.

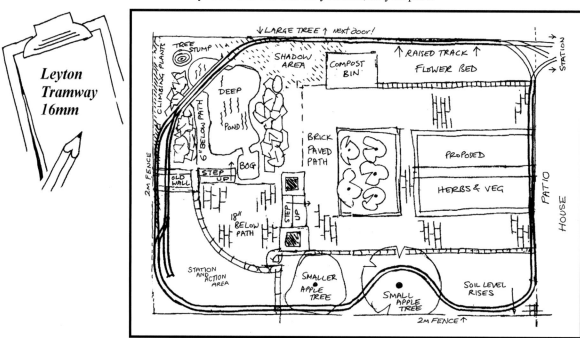

*Leyton Tramway 16mm*

Surveying the garden should result in at least one good ground plan. This should also show the position of tree trunks and shrubs. A few vital measurements and some graph paper or with a big and complex railway, sticks in the ground making one metre squares. A most useful assistance is to take photographs, which often reveal things that we just do not notice ordinarily. They also give us a chance to actually draw the railway onto the pictures of the garden. It is much cheaper to have little photo prints colour photocopied up to A4 size for this purpose. The best procedure for photo prints that you can use, is to hold the camera as level as possible and make (six photos) a joined up 360 degree panorama of the garden.

Conifers will shed needles, others will shed resin and Sycamores send 'windmill' seeds down all Winter. Some trees cause a black scum to form underneath them. This can stick to wheels. Large leaves, from chestnuts are not a problem, small leaves or pine needles become wedged into points. Sycamore pods on sleepers uncouple wagons. We need to be aware just what trees and shrubs drip resin or rain, and where, so that we can avoid them, or run in a tunnel beneath them!

The need for track cleaning - for electrical pick-up may even be so serious as to point us towards battery power if we plan badly in the early stages. Live steam does not require quite as much cleaning, and though locos may be heavy, light wagons can derail from dirty, debris covered tracks – or crosswinds. High sided empty plastic boxcars- I use up to 300gms of 'ballast' fixed inside over each bogie.

You can see that a whole world of study can open up to us if we wish to acquire new expertise. We could look at geology, topography, gain a new insight into garden horticulture, and combine all of this into surveying and garden design. The railway will certainly expand our horizons. We are following in some mighty footsteps. This can prove to be far more than just a train set outside.

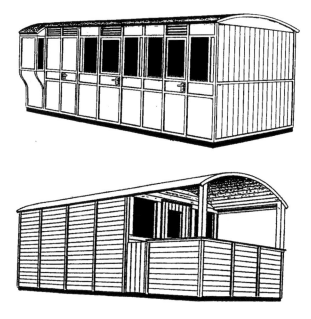

**You can have a garden shed that looks like a guard's van or carriage. Prices start at a reasonble level. Watch your trains from a train?**

# Fifteen Feet by Twenty
## On an apartment roof timber deck

*Once upon a time 'decking' was the stuff sailors stood on. Recently the fashion has been to cover any outdoor ground space with designer timber, slavishly following favourite gardening (gardening?) television programmes and their use of hard landscaping. When I was called upon to provide tracks on a 'Titchmarsh' style 4Mx5M timber deck I thought the result would be simply an outdoor trainset. I was mistaken.*

**The planning stage.
Though this was a simple deck structure, it still had obstacles, obstructions, and the owner had definite ideas for his railway layout.
There was also a massive sculpture to be negotiated.**

The timber deck covered the terrace of a roof top penthouse overlooking London. The area, about the same size as many patios and small back gardens, was to provide a running area for the owner's handsome Bockholt Gauge-1 trains.

Because they are so close to the prototypes, the length is the obvious feature. Fully operational in every way, bogie wagons are 700mm long. Though made to the highest display quality, Bockholts are made to run – outside if need be. They can cost over ten thousand pounds. You could retire early and raid your pension fund. If the government's taken that already, become a charity and apply to the lottery.

This all caused a great number of challenges. The size of the deck restricted the widest curve radius – round the perimeter, to 2.2Metres (garden narrow gauge curves sometimes are as tight as 0.8M). I assumed that the problem would be the long wheelbases of the locomotives, which included two decapods. It wasn't. The real difficulty appeared later. The loco pony trucks would not move far enough sideways to follow even a slightly misaligned curve. The wagon bogies also had a restriction on their pivots, though the holes were elongated sideways.

### Because the track would be under the minimum specified curve, there was no room at all for play in track laying.

The deck timber was not flat everywhere, and twisted in places. All of this impinged upon the four or five millimetre tolerance available on the running gear. The largest locomotive had sprung doors to the cab, and these would bind with the tender.

**These are the clearances that we laid our G-Scale tracks.**
**It pays to do this exercise before you begin, using your longest, widest rolling stock.**
**Bockholt are long, but Gauge-1 is narrow compared to G-Scale and 16mm.**

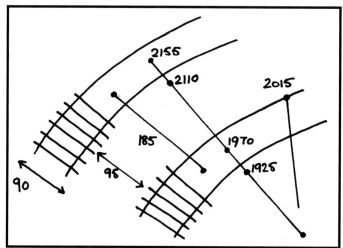

At the end of the first day we had laid two tracks, about 50Metres in total The Bockholts did stay on the rails - when they were tested at reasonable speeds. The tracks were fixed with Phillips self-tapping screws.

I started using string and chalk to set the required curves radii, but the rain washed the marks away. On the second try I used a fabric tape measure pinned to the 'centre' and marked each sleeper position as I laid track. Now I cut a plywood template a couple of metres curve length. Push the track tight to this and nail it down. The tape measure circle was much more consistent, as is my plywood template system.

I had hoped for a hot day to set the rail gaps to minimum (zero) but the weather variations meant difficulties. The track went from shade to full sun, then the sun disappeared altogether. Brass does move a great deal. The Tenmille sleepers have holes in the centre but this often fell at the gap between deck timbers. I pinned at the outside.

The track input wires were soldered to fishplates before fitting, easier than trying to solder to a big strip of brass rail heatsink outdoors. The fishplates were filled with copper grease. A quick meter measurement everywhere showed no current drop anywhere, though the locos slowed down considerably at curves due to friction, indicating wear potential, on the rails because the wheels are steel.

Lastly, some buildings were added to provide the village served by the Pola Schonweiler station. The new railway had a purpose.

**Oh, and there was a tree. Split the tracks? This would make the inner track even tighter radius.**
**Not as simple as I first thought.**

I included this railway because there are similaritites with planning and installing a track on a patio. Flagstone slabs can be uneven, and there are always tubs and planters that can or cannot be moved.

*We did run around the Barbara Hepworth sculpture, her pieces were meant to be seen outdoors too.*

This railway as built even has interesting 'reverse curves' – the transition into major curves as found on main lines laid for speed,, and proved to be not just two parallel tracks on a 'Ground Force' deck, but in the village centre there is a Charlie Dimmock style water feature!

# 4. Getting Started

*The romantic nature of steam trains continues to engage young and old alike, from the film Brief Encounter, set on Carnforth Station, now under restoration by the Railway Heritage Trust, to Thomas, and the Hogwarts Express in the Harry Potter best selling childrens' books. Modelling railways more than stands the test of time in toy shops where the model railway section attracts fathers and grandfathers as well as youngsters.*

The indoor railway scene is still dominated by the continuing Hornby 'OO' but few realise that 'big – scale' trains can be had for similar money. Starter sets in small indoor and large outdoor scales are almost the same price.

The added attraction is that garden design, horticulture – mostly miniature planting and rockeries, and in this modern world, electronic controls, are all peripheral interests and activities. Which means whole family involvement. Children can purchase pocket money train accessories - or plants. Round the rockery, trains can be models of rack railways like the ones in Switzerland, and a knowledge of Alpines and small leafed herbs is useful.

**The railway can be incorporated behind a boundary wall feature. Here, a paved area with seats and a viewing arch built into the wall. Planting, and pots soften the hard full sized bricks.**

To enhance the realism of the trains, miniature planting near the tracks is a must. Expresses can traverse a pond at high speed, emitting realistic digital sound on a magnificent model viaduct. This could provide more ongoing involvement than a plastic 'water feature' and half a dozen goldfish. Saturdays can be spent at the model shop – or the garden centre.

**Simplest track base is shovel wide, plastic lined, ballast stones filled trench. Track sits on smooth mortar about 2cms thick, or blocks. Groundcover hides hard edges.**

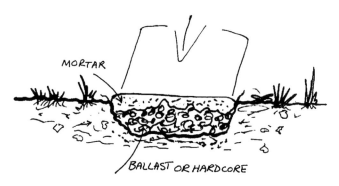

MORTAR

BALLAST OR HARDCORE

Garden railway owners are quite coy about their enthusiasm, and range to Sir William McAlpine running real trains from real stations through real tunnels at his Henley estate. In the 1930's so did Herman Goring on his estate at Karinhal. Walt

Disney collected locomotives and built ride-on railways at each Disney Park. Disney World in Orlando overshadows 'The Train Station' where a small 'Porter' steam loco pulls a train in a circle around a building housing the largest big-scale display in the USA, built by retired Delton Locoworks owner Bob Schuster.

### *Pete Waterman, 'Pop Idol' guru, owns real locomotives, leases them on our main lines, and models 'O' scale railways.*

Deputy Prime Minister John Prescott's son is a G-Scale collector. So is the son of Laura Ashley. Frank Sinatra was an avid rail fan. Perhaps some of us have travelled on a miniature railway owned by Sir Billy Butlin?

You can have your garden shed made to look like a signal box, but gardeners seldom have time to sit and contemplate their works, preferring to be active outdoors

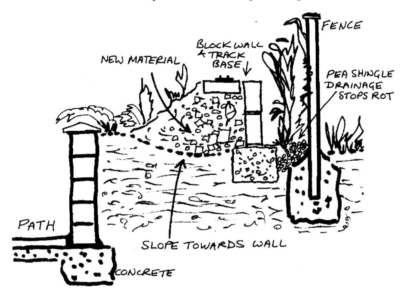

**Typical raised track using insulating lightweight blocks. Wall and shingle drain protect the fence. Track will screw to block bed.**

How much better, to view your garden *from* your garden railway.
 Still in the garden, but much larger, is the 'one inch to the foot' gauge with trains that you can ride on, popular in the U.S.A. A sixteen meter circle of five inch gauge tracks, (in the U.S.A. 4 ¾ inches) a battery powered loco and two 'sit on' wagons for a few thousand pounds gets you started at this size. A whole railway for the price of a designer garden seat?

**What's next The Grand Canyon?**

**Saltash Bridge spans the Meon river in deepest Hampshire. Richard has several others too.**

19.

To make a garden railway integrate with a garden can include feats of engineering if we so wish. I have built several ponds, one thirty feet across, so that a suspension bridge had to be devised to carry the trains, while underneath model boats could pass. The owner of a garden railway in Hampshire has several viaducts, and a ten metre long by two metre high model of the Saltash bridge " a necessity" he claims, across a river. There are tales of a scale Forth Bridge tucked away in a large garden……..

It's worth repeating, the true garden railway should be integrated into the surroundings. When Brunel planned 'God's Wonderful Railway' he set off in a pony and trap to survey his GWR line from London to Bristol. He embelished the countryside that his railway traversed. Around Bath you can see his work blending, even enhancing that lovely city as the line snakes through tunnels and bridges. His major tunnel, the huge opening in the hillside at Box (for his eight foot broad gauge trains) is still there, and it is no accident, though it may be a conceit, that the sun shines straight through this long dark tube around his birthday.

A simple railway in a private garden can take as little as a weekend to three weeks before the first train starts its journey. Large commercial ventures can take weeks to install. All our efforts take at least one or two seasons to grow to maturity.

Garden Railways can match the size of your pocket, and take years of attention. Just as a garden grows, so does a garden railway. However, the planning, or the building, or the horticulture, will each have their own fascination and importance, either for the 'owner' of the line, or members of the family. The railway, the garden, and the family can grow together as mine did.

**Trackbase laid direct in existing beds . This is one end of a dog-bone single line with return loops. Tomorrow it will be ready for tracks.**

*We have had glass, chrome, mirrors, painted concrete, even a signal box garden, so I have hopes to build the first integrated railway garden at Chelsea Flower Show.*

The increasing demand for garden railway design/building skills that prompted my books and DVDs has led to my e-mail and postal D.I.Y. consulting business because almost half of newcomers to the hobby simply need a helping hand to get started in the midst of the overwhelming choices. All the world's trains are readily available off the shelf, with tank engined starter sets at around a hundred pounds running on 18volts 5 amps, right up to real steam locos at five hundred pounds and fired by butane. Control is by the ubiquitous 'turn a knob' box, wireless digital, or 'standard' radio control - as used for model cars and aeroplanes.

Yes, there are models of the Indian 'Darjeeling' Himalayan Railway, The Orient Express, Virgin trains HST - 4 metres long (a starter set) and of course the Flying Scotsman locomotive, Gauge-1, nearly a metre long, made in Japan, real fire, real steam, real smoke - real smell!

## A Rockery Railway in a Weekend

*So, Spring is here, your garden has the fountain water feature, the gazebo, the deck area and patio? What project for this season?*
*A model railway, designed to run outdoors, whatever the weather, will add movement, sound, and interest. That circle of track on the lawn really should be integrated.*

What better place to run our railway than round a rockery? This can involve bridges and tunnels. So, here we have a step by simple step guide to that rockery you've always promised yourself, or the wife.

Because we are going to make quite a heap of heavy stone, we need to check out the ground that will be covered. Make sure there are no drains underneath. A good idea is to remove a foot or so of topsoil for planting use later. This should get us down to a more stable load-bearing layer. The starter set tracks will probably form a circle about three metres in diameter so I suggest that the rockery is a little larger, with the tracks about half a metre up off ground level.

To complete this fairly simple project in a weekend, all the materials, and some labour will need to be on hand at the start, and you will need a good plan. The weather does not matter.

A good 'base' is a heap of hardcore, otherwise any convenient mound of material that will not subside in the rain (such as topsoil would). This is a good time to get rid of all that old rubbish and also import some hardcore.

The question of rocks will no doubt occur to us as we look at our growing heap, four metres in diameter and a couple in height. The local garden centre may charge you up to five pounds a lump for their little rocks. Much better, is to contact the nearest quarry. Every county in the British Isles has its own local stone. Some gardens might have bedrock, with a wafer thin covering of topsoil. Use Yellow Pages for this part of the construction.

A rockery of the size we are contemplating here would need about a ton of lumps. This would give twenty pieces, each about a hundredweight - just liftable. A little larger and you need strong help – and a large wheel barrow. The quarry truck that delivers to your nearest garden centre might drop off a ton for under a hundred pounds.

A good method is to build two or three stepped circles, filling in the pyramid with hardcore, and topping off with a nice arrangement of interesting pieces as you build. If you wished that you had a particular shape rock, you can make your own. Dig a hole about a shovel sized square, and deep. Fill this with a mixture of cement to four parts sand/grit, and two parts compost. When this has set after a few days, remove the lump from the ground. This is 'Hypatufa' and makes excellent fake big rocks, that quickly support moss. Bare lumps can be encouraged to grow moss by painting with yoghurt, or liquid manure. If the rockery is out of sight, urine works well too! Along the way, we can fix rocks in place with mortar (24 hours to set) or for speed, use gap filling expanding DIY foam. (read the can carefully, you need a water spray).

***This simple circle could remain as a track for the children or visitors, even when you move on to grander things.***

**Above; GRS Wisbeech & Upwell tram loco emerges from a dummy tunnel**

**Of course, you can always go straight over the rockery rocks. This railway models Snowdon. LGB Ballenberg loco and detailing bits from GRS.**

Most Alpines and many small plants require sharp drainage and will thrive in 'planting pockets' of soil and grit (saxifrage, Corsican mint, thyme). You can even leave them in their pots. There are opportunities for perfume too. Some plants, such as Corsican Mint will give off scent when brushed by a train. What we need are cracks and crevices between our rocks. We can fill larger areas with the removed topsoil and plant small leafed shrubs. We also have a use for (real) dwarf conifers and low ground cover, like cotoneaster.

Laying our railway track, I suggest a (4:1 sand/cement) mortar base. This needs to be troweled smooth and level, with no slopes over 1 in 40 or our train will slide in morning dew or rain. Roughly level is best. If necessary, the tracks can be masonry nailed down, or fixed with outdoor/bathroom mastic of some kind.

You might put a tunnel here and there. The very young can run their 'Playmobil' trains straight on our tracks – which can be walked on for maintenance and gardening – so they can do no damage.

**Give it time! The trains are all running after a long hard weekend's work for the whole family.**

**Two 'rockeries in a weekend'.**

If you have the hardcore and rocks to hand, a long weekend will see the trains running and give you the quiet chuff-chuff of a train in the distance on that Summer evening.

This five by five metre circle rockery railway in a corner of the garden was completed with trains running after a long weekend's work. The foreground track will later extend to make the other end of a dog-bone *(see previous pictures)*. Meanwhile, it's the bottom circle here.

The two lines going out at bottom right join up, for trains to run up onto high level and into or out of 'night store' shed. High level track is a loop from the shed over far LGB bridge just out and back for now.

# 5. Construction

## Bridges and Tunnels

*Metal, wood or stone? The great railway engineers used whatever was to hand. They were also modest. Most engineering structures blend into the landscape, and their simplicity belies the genius of the designer.*

We do not have the same size of problem, but we are still "building a real railway in the real world". We must make good foundations that withstand frost, ice, rain and sun. Typically, I find clay the worst. It bakes hard in summer when it shrinks as the water evaporates. In Winter or rain, the clay swells and can become a 'fluidised bed' moving like sand. The answer is the same as for a 'real' structure – go deep. A couple of feet down and we may miss all but the most prolonged rain and sun.

A study of some of the most famous bridge designs (if it interests you) will actually solve our miniature problems for us!

Because we need our structures to last for a few years or more, we should really let a rockery or garden feature that we have built, stand over a Winter at least before we build a piece of railway engineering on it.  This will let it settle.

Most bridges will benefit if the below ground footings (a couple of concrete blocks at each end) for the abutments are made in this way.  Please make the abutments - from which any bridge must spring - look correct. I have seen so many bridges rest on normal house-bricks that just look wrong and spoil the whole effect.

Another 'real world' device, is to place a very large weight where our foundation area is to go. Let this overwinter, then start foundations the next season.

Normally our bridges will only have to carry a 'scale' weight, in G-Scale, the most popular, a train will weigh 20 kilos or so. For a small bridge, a live steam loco

**G64 Gauge 3 Pannier and concrete viaduct from GRS blends well into this lawn edge. Mortar or car body filler and foam fill in the arches for a quick build.**
*(Photo GRS)*

300mm long  might weigh 5 kilos. Two locos passing – 10kilos. However, we might need to traverse the bridge ourselves to reach parts of the track. There are no calculation tables available for us. However, as a guide, I have built a reinforced

(with chicken wire) concrete arch spanning a metre, and about 3cms thick, between two concrete block abutments, that I could walk over – after about six months. Concrete becomes stronger with age.

**Moulded concrete is an under used material, and the fact that it is 'plastic' till it sets seems to have escaped many engineers.**

We can make a mould in fibreglass or rubber and cast viaduct sections, or walls. Customised tunnel portals are often made this way using clay for the 'master', from which a latex mould is made.

**For speed, I use expanding adhesive foam. When it's set hide it or paint it grey/black/stone colour.**
**A small tunnel in half an hour.**

I mentioned wood and stone. Timber merchants supply hardwood pieces about 1 centimeter square by a couple of meters long. This is an excellent material for trestle bridge construction, carrying quite heavy weights over individual spans of a metre or so. The wood can be weather treated and last for some years.
This is also about the scale size of trestle viaducts designed by Brunel which rested on stone pillars.

**GRS sectional viaduct in concrete. Fixed together with 'Padding'. Foamed over the cardboard inserts, foam cut with a long kitchen knife to shape the arches. Mortar track base on top.**

Viaducts are a particular problem. A viaduct on a curve is the most difficult, and to see this done really well makes a railway come alive. Garden Railway Specialists supply a wide range of concrete engineering components, from retaining walls to tunnel portals and wooden viaduct pillars.

Metal bridges are an off the shelf purchase, even to your own designs. GRS have 4 types. Like other real bridges they may need weatherproofing paint applied. Spans of two meters are possible.

Luckily we do not have to bore tunnels ourselves. We can 'build' tunnels that look like the real thing. The favourite method is 'cut-and-cover'. This was much used for the larger London underground lines near the surface, and the 14 track exit from grand central station in New York.

**Embankment built up with slate chips and stony clay, supported by rocks. Track base is mortar. Not yet finished or planted, test trains seem OK.**

My system is easy. Place a garden paving slab on the ground as the tunnel base, place two concrete blocks, one each side, and another slab on top of these. They can be mortared into position if needed. A slight slope will also help drainage.

The 'mountain' can then be added above this tunnel. For a longer tunnel, more sections can be added, but leave spaces between. They can be camouflaged away. We must be able to reach into a tunnel for we are almost certain to attract hibernating or nesting wildlife.

This tunnel space will take our weight, and is large enough for double lines up to G-Scale, and to accommodate a curve. Spray paint the inside black, and the finishing portal at the entrance will give little clue to the size of the cavern inside.

### *Tunnels can be very useful in supplying an element of surprise!*

**Not exactly a surprise – the worst place to have a derailment. When the lid is on this part of the track, and it's raining, I bet there will be a derailment. Never have a tunnel longer than you can reach into.**

Trains can disappear and reappear. A whistle sounds so much better echoing through a tunnel, and the sound unit could be built into the tunnel rather than on board the loco. A whistle unit from Maplin or Radio Shack can be track fed and a reed switch thrown by a loco magnet.

Before we leave bridges, this may be the best place to raise the topic of loading gauge again. All railways must determine their loading gauge at an early stage. By fixing the maximum height and width, the minimum curves can be determined (long carriages will overhang in the middle) and all the clearances, at tunnels and bridges will be fixed. In the U.S.A. the loading gauge is larger than Europe, so the trains are higher, and wider. The tracks farther apart.

The GWR loading gauge allowed locomotive cylinders to stick out sideways farther that on the LNER. When locomotives were exchanged at various times, and at the end of steam, platform edges were damaged, and caused damage to locos.
It is advisable to ask for the dimensions of the most popular model manufacturers and take the largest in the list. These are measurements that we never are given – how high? How wide? How long between bogie pivots? Most of us believe we will never run a certain loco or wagon, but this precludes visitors, or that most popular pastime, our railway extensions and developments.

## Construction - Materials

*When we model the stations, platforms, railway cottages, water towers, coal stores, freight handling depots, bridges, embankments – even little people to populate our miniature world – we must be aware that we model out of doors, with all that nature can throw at us, from frost to moles.*
*The making of models that will be used and even remain out of doors is unique to our hobby, yet little information is provided or gathered for us.*

Some of the modern construction materials are not so weather resistant. Plywood is readily available and is offered in several "grades". Usually we try for the most expensive – 'marine ply' on the assumption that it is waterproof. The grades denote the glue specification, prolonged immersion or wetting will 'de-laminate' any ply. In boats, it is always protected from water contact. When the material is protected

**16mm end of line with turntable and holes for tanks with water.**
**This will be a beautifully modelled canal scene that can only enhance an afternoon on the patio.**
**See later picture - almost finished.**
*R.McMahon*

then a long life can be expected. Another sheet material, and much cheaper, is 'Stirlingboard', looking like large chips of wood compressed into a large sheet, this is much used for flat roofs where it will be covered up by thick layers of roofing felt. Plastic sofit boards and bits for track edgings, new waterproof chipboards are useful. We should use only waterproof fixings, glue, and screws. Wood should always be 'Tanalised' – (green preservatives containing copper) that is, pressure treated against rot, or coated with some sort of preservative (creosote- contains phenol and attacks some plastic sleepers).

Our trains are either made of metals – brass, white metal, stainless steel, bronze – or of plastics – ABS, Lexan, Luran S, Styrene. The greatest threat to our models is not rain, wind or frost but the sun and its ultra-violet rays, plus the baking heat that we sometimes let our models endure.

Many of our suppliers, LGB in particular, take great notice of the outdoor nature of our hobby. You will see "Drinnen und Draussen" indoors and outside, on their boxes, but not all of them. Track reed switches are not 'puddle proof'.

### They often paint on top of the coloured plastic. Why? To give extra ultraviolet protection.

The plastic itself, in the case of LGB, is Luran-S, a polycarbonate plastic that meets environmental standards for temperatures from –40C to +100C. Many models are injection moulded in ABS, the same plastic is used for the exterior parts of motor cars. Some model buildings are cast in polyester resin, the same as all those fibreglass boats bobbing about in marinas.

Other hobbies with outdoor scale modelling fall into the boat, 'plane or racing car categories. These models are carefully built and operated when the weather is favourable (to the modeller), otherwise they are transported carefully and kept in special cases or displayed – indoors. Our trains can run better in the wet or snow!

We use a great deal of their technologies. Electric motors, not just to power locomotives- we leave point motors fixed to the track bed for years. We use electronics for sound or auto-shuttle train operation. We use radio control units,

either basic go/stop or complex digital running of several trains and operated accessories.

**Above; wheel wear after a season's daily running. Grooves in wheels, Plate contacts worn. Spring wheel contacts OK.**

**There are many ways to lay tracks. This is just my preferred way. Lifting after four years proved easy. Mortar bed, fishtank gravel 5mm or less and quick set mortar. Track fixed with nails. The screwdriver lifts. The lump hammer knocked the wall down.**

We started in this hobby to run trains, so for many of us the construction itself may be a relaxation, and enjoyable, but few will establish a track bed one season, then wait till next year to put down the rails, yet this is what we should do. We want our construction to progress to 'tracks open' as quickly as possible. We can use 'Quick setting mortar" – really a resin, and yes it's fast.

Traditional construction can also incorporate some new technology. Car body filler (resin putty) is a good adhesive except on a frosty day, will set in minutes.

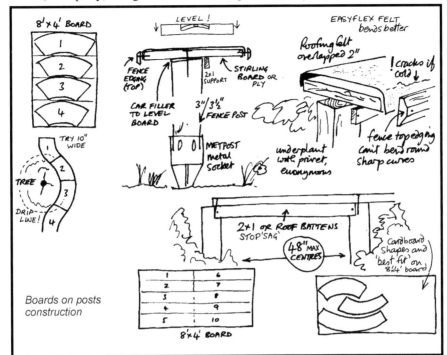

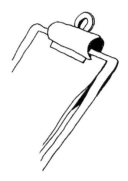

**Track base on posts for Gauge-1 layouts. Interlink make this in metal as a bolt together system 'Track Up'**

This can hold tracks in place when we bend a curve. Like the gap filling foam, it sticks to (dry) cement, it is not waterproof but will set under water.

There are variations of epoxy glues. These are usually two-part. That is they will have a glue and a 'hardener' or 'accelerator'. Some will set overnight, others claim to set in five minutes. These will glue some soft plastics and many metals. They are waterproof but ultraviolet light can breakdown the bond. Epoxy glues will fix white cast metal detailing on a model locomotive. They are used to glue the aluminium 'skin' on aircraft.

For metal model kits and wires, (tin/lead and variations) solder is the main joining method. Usually with a gas soldering iron bonding outdoor track joins with (thick) copper or aluminium wire for electrical continuity.

### Ask a sailor, bonding tin/lead and brass, copper, aluminium plus acid water causes corrosion.

Some years ago, an accident in a laboratory resulted in 'Superglue' named because it will glue skin together, and has been widely used for this purpose by surgeons

and schoolchildren. Superglue also has many variants, from clear liquid to thick, and while they started out as instant, with no antidote, there are now slower setting and release agents available. Superglues have a slight achilles heal . and can turn white when moisture is near.

Superglues work on most materials (even leather) and give a high strength bond in seconds,

In modelling, we often try to fix a piece of unknown plastic to a piece of unknown metal.

This would be a challenge for any adhesive. Copper, tin, bronze will inhibit polyesters and prevent curing of resins. Even stainless steel has an 'active' state, when air is excluded it can corrode.

Most of the time we have to have a 'menu' of glues at hand. Sometimes it is possible to fix a glue to one component, another to a second, then bond those two glues. Under some conditions, epoxy and superglue will do this without either breaking its own bond.

### Out of doors, heat is conducted away rapidly by long lengths of metal - the railway tracks.

All outdoor railway modellers will agree, the hobby has brought them new knowledge and skills, from electrics to horticulture.

For this reason, most railways have a workshop of some sort, and it should be available before the railway construction work begins.

*Technology based construction materials in the 21$^{st}$ century allow us to do anything – literally. I have not seen a railway through a tunnel under a pond – but I know there must be one somewhere.*

## Construction - Water

*In the same way that fountains and water features are advertised – to give movement in the garden, I am constantly surprised that no one has ever shown a railway to give interest and added movement. Garden Centres, the television and magazines on gardening ignore us completely.*

One of the prime reasons for putting anything in the garden is to give distraction.

The more areas of interest, the more interesting the garden. We are all aware through television programmes, that we can have 'interest' all the year round by judicious planting. The interest is horticultural and provided by seasonal flowerings and colours. A plain area of lawn soon becomes boring to view.

Railway engineering and water are great challenges, and can provide satisfaction and enjoyment with the solution of problems that the two present together. A simple pond can become an obstacle that must be rounded or bridged.

Many railways run along sea walls – The SNCF at the Cote D'Azure past Nice, the Western region at Teignmouth and Dawlish. River valleys (Glyn Valley Tramway) are a welcome feature for the railway builder.

We can emulate some of the civil engineer's solutions in our garden and provide visual interest by taking our railway around or over a stretch of water. Here we have a bridge and pump in a tank at bottom to give a waterfall effect. Switch on post at right activates train and pump.

There are several G-Scale model boats, from canal barges (GRS) to Coastguard and trawlers (Snetterton). Limit yours to three, or you'll have more than the Royal Navy and have to become a country.

Many modern ponds will have Butyl liners. These rubber membranes can be punctured. We may wish to span some water with a bridge that needs supports rising from the surface. The safest way will be to place a sheet of expanded polystyrene (Jablite) *under* the lining material, and another sheet above, this sandwich protects the liner and a concrete block on top of the two will form an excellent foundation under the water for any construction.

### Remember that we must reach all parts of our railway for maintenance. A small boat may be needed!

The 'sandwich' system allows us to build waterside docks and even islands that the railway can employ in its tracklaying.

**You don't need a lot of water.**

**Finished 16mm canal dockside scene built on wooden base. Note plastic 'sofit' as backboard.**

*R.McMahon.*

If the water area is large enough, it works well to build a wall at one edge in this manner, then fill in behind, again on top of the liner, and incorporate the railway along the edge. This allows us to modify our water's edge planting so that we can use small leaved and dwarf 'marginals' planting in keeping with the railway's size and scale.

Waterfalls and moving water will demand further hydraulic skills from the serious builder. The simplest waterfall into a pond can be made with overlapping pieces of liner. I have not managed to permanently paint black butyl rubber. These run downhill so that water stays where we plan. Then rocks, boulders or whatever mountainous terrain we conceive, can be assembled on this in the knowledge that we will not simply pump water out of the pond to run away. Concrete is water permeable but O.K. for waterfalls and streams.

Less visible than a black butyl liner, is fibreglass laid on the ground. The fibreglass matt is spread and resin applied to form a watercourse that we may bridge later. The fibreglass has the property to look like water if it is at all visible.

Whatever we do, it will help if the water is moving. Just like our trains, there is something restful and engaging about the tinkling sound of running water on a

Summer's afternoon. This implies that a pump will be needed. There are many pond pumps available, with adequate safety features. My personal preference is to use boat bilge pumps. These run on twelve volts and consume a reasonably small current, such as we are used to in railway practice generally. Most bilge pumps are not rated for continuous use so it is advisable to check this out.

The automotive industry also uses many types of pump – for petrol, and windscreen washers. These are all twelve volt operating for cars.

Larger pumps will be needed for any but the smallest waterfalls or 'lion's head' wall spouts, and these are almost certain to be the type that builders use to empty holes in the ground. These are re-packaged for garden centres as units with many fittings for fountains. They will usually specify the amount of water pumped, in gallons per hour, and the height to which it can be pumped, as for instance 'two meters head'. A holding tank, usually an old household water tank of thirty gallons or so will provide a suitable 'buffer' at the high end, or in the case of a false stream, at the receiving end where the pump will return it via a 3/4inch garden hose up to the origin.

**SNCF Mikado loco with steam sound hauls an LGB Orient Express with lighted dining and sleeping cars across ten metres wide water, Merrivale.**

Planning rockeries near water, and incorporating water will provide the railway with many engineering challenges. The final scene, reflected in a pond can be further enhanced by the model railway features.

### *A word of caution, smaller children can come to harm in only inches of water in minutes.*

You should build in safety features that prevent access for little ones such as thick planting, a wide shallow slope at the edge (helps wildlife out), or a wall. Larger ponds - either an indication of depth, so that adults know they can wade in, or larger still, a small plastic dinghy, which is also useful for maintenance and planting. A life ring isn't such a bad idea.

A last point. We do have serious rainfall in the northern hemisphere and a pond can easily overflow. It is advisable to decide in advance where this water will go and incorporate an overflow pipe at the water level or just above. It is possible in some cases and with local permissions, to route drainpipe rain water into ponds so that dry Summers do not affect pond levels too much. (Today in most areas, it is not permissible to put rainwater into waste water pipes (the drains) and most rainwater downpipes go to 'soakaways' (large pits full of stones at about five meters from the house). We should look carefully at drainage for our railway, and whether it may block rainwater run-off from our garden or lawn.

# 6. Track

## Track types and compatibility

*We live in a consumer society, and expect choice in everything. Sometimes we have too many choices? Just as there are horses for courses, our plan may well determine what kind of track we need. This may even narrow our choices for us. There are several main track systems available to us. Not all have a full range of bits and pieces, and the choice is highly subjective – it's your railway.*

Most suppliers will have the usual straights and curves, in a variety of radii. However, the fewer joins the better, especially if we are looking for electrical continuity. So my recommendation would be the longer one metre or 1500mm lengths. These usually come in 'flexible' format and even unassembled, cheaper. I don't make tighter curves than I can buy, tightly bent track easily goes out of gauge.

### *The machine-cut ends of rails are always sharp, and need de-burring. Filing saves wear on sliding pickups and running gear.*

Because I have a 'manly' shaped waist. I bend flexible track round me and this gives a gentle curve you understand. Others bend incrementally round a knee.
This is a little unscientific and so I have used rail benders as well as track benders. Difficult in the rain, handheld, trackside. They go rusty too. I always have some curved track pieces available to get me out of trouble in a hurry.

Our track is usually very hard brass, but stainless steel is available. (still needs cleaning). The LGB profile is meant to be that of a narrow gauge line, though these would have randomly spaced sleepers (as Peco G45 does). Another subtle difference between manufacturers is rail to sleeper height (web height). With Tenmille for one, being shallower than LGB. This means that LGB track switches (reed switches) may be at the wrong height for loco magnets to trigger them.

### *Never, ever, have any projection above the rail height between the rails (the 'four-foot'). Overall rail on sleeper height can vary too – affecting your loading gauge.*

Peco 'Streamline' Gauge-1 track is 1: 30 scale, G45 'narrow gauge, 1:22.5.
**LGB track joins to Aristo, USA Trains and Accucraft.**

G-scale 'standard gauge' is 64mm between the rails.
Tenmille 1 to Peco, serious modification of the fishplates.
Tenmille G to LGB , very difficult.
Tenmille G to Peco G – not possible.

I may have said elsewhere that over time, manufacturers change the profile and flanges of the wheels fitted to models. Each track manufacturer is different again. This does not usually cause trouble, except at points. Changes to the centrepiece and the 'frogs' or blades, can cause havoc with derailments for no apparent reason.

**Watching mortar set?**

**The television trackbase is hardening. Useful track pieces are used to plan and position curves accurately. It's handy to have some of these rather than attempt to bend 'Flexitrack' to tight radius.**

**Next day we will be track laying and fixing, with some planting trackside.**

## Track Laying

*There are as many variations in the preparation for track laying, as there are railways. The reason for planning our railway, as far as we can, before commencing is so that we can provide a good support for the track, which will sit on top of our prepared base – the 'formation. We hope that it will not deform, flood, subside, or slip away after heavy rain. We do not want our (heavy) station building to crack or collapse onto the track after subsidence.*

 Track is probably going to be the most expensive of our purchases, and is cheaper bought in bulk. There is a case for laying a small length to try out our skills in construction. I advise garden railway builders to lay a straight or circle first, if there is one in their plan somewhere. Otherwise the impetus and interest, of the family as well, will be lost while everyone waits for the track to be able to accept a train.  .

We must lay our track, then build our stations, so that the train can run into the platform not run INTO the platform. Clearances everywhere are crucial.

The most favoured 'ground based' track bed systems involve digging a trench.
I was taken by surprise when I saw the television programme planned for this topic showing a trench about a foot deep and wide, filled with reinforced concrete – to take just a single G-scale line! Worse, I read an article in a magazine that suggested *reinforced* concrete for 'OO' in the garden. They were joking….weren't they?

### There are probably as many track-base methods as there are railway builders.

A trench lined with polythene and filled with 'ballast' (25mm stones) and/or insulating building blocks laid flat on their sides will make an excellent 'formation'. This gives us a flat, stable surface that should stay weed free, does not flood (holes in the polythene), and that we can walk on. Frequently the only way to reach all parts of our track is to walk along it. This 'trough' can be simple and easy to make. Properly constructed, and not a lot wider than the track, it should not really be visible. Double tracks need about ten inches. The track will rest on top, and in the interests of realism, seem to be held in place by scale ballast.

We could possibly use bricks or blocks at half meter intervals, 'wriggled' down level and held by ballast. If we use blocks, we can screw the track directly to them.

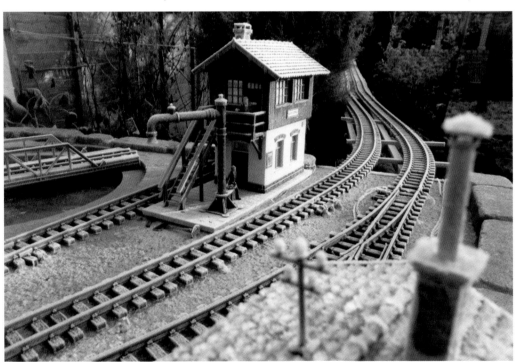

Using builders' ballast, it will help to use smaller stones (pea shingle) on top, then mortar mix to give the flat track - bed we need. I use a very long (4M tile batten) piece of wood to remove 'humps'. This 'foundation' will extend sideways under other constructions - we may have only a centimetre clearance in our loading gauge.

In reality ballast is made of sharp granite chips, with sharp shapes that lock together, and hold the track in place. Otherwise it would be dragged forward by a thousand ton train braking for a station, or moved sideways as an express rounds a curve at speed. My tracks are usually nailed- against theft. Ballast is cosmetic.
I use aquarium gravel that is close to the real thing in scale about 2mm size. Horticultural grit tends to be a little large at about 6mm in my opinion. Anything

5mm to dust is good. To hold this in place against the ravages of bird attack I use 'quick setting mortar', really a kind of resin. Then water spray or allow dew to set.

Others use PVA liquid glue to stabilise their preference, though this can turn white in the rain. LGB also have a 'sponge' type of roadbed ballast system for their preshaped track pieces.

**My 'traditional' method is handed on.
Mortar base with masonry nailed track is ballasted with 5mm grit and rapid sand/cement mix.
The spray will set this hard in minutes and overnight dew fix it to the base.
Paintbrush is used to shape the mix to a shoulder at sleeper ends following proper railway practice in steam days.
Sun Inn tracks are now four years old.**

Never underestimate the dangers of the real world and wildlife attacks. Moles will tunnel under your foundations and eat anything that looks like a root or worm – wires. Birds will peck at their reflection in the windows of model buildings. Badgers will eat signals, and red wire (worms again) Family pets, often other people's - hailstones probably cause the most damage .

For these reasons, I believe that G-scale and Gauge 3 are well chosen for garden railways. Their size and weight are of great benefit. The collision between a snail and a '00' flying Scotsman could be fatal – for the locomotive!

Well secured trackwork is important  because we will have a large sum of money laying on the ground in the form of brass rail. The garden  blowers for leaves can be used to clear the tracks after Winter . I do not recommend the suction setting. One railroader removed all the little people before he could switch off.

The permanence of your 'permanent way' may concern you if you might sell in a few years but most properly integrated  railways leave little or no scar  when they are removed, and with proper construction in the first place this should not be a problem . Rockeries, and their planting can remain to enhance the landscape and this goes for properly installed water features too.
You may be transplanting your railway at a later date. Most modern trackwork properly installed, is easy to release from its track bed and move to a new site with little loss. The best fixing method, if a move or extension is a possibility, is to screw the track down driving 'self tapping' screws directly into an insulating block, or with plug fixings into brick. I have lifted track ten years old with no problems.

So far, I have seldom run track on posts.  However, many modellers, particularly Gauge-1, use the method. The ability to run alongside a live steam model that is not radio controlled is essential. Garden Centers have many fencing accessories. Metal sockets driven into the ground, holding the posts, seem a good system. The actual track bed, even if  'marine plywood' (meaning the glue is marine, not the wood) needs to be kept dry. A topping of roofing felt (Easyflex is good), taken round the sides and fixed underneath or with side pieces will do the trick, and looks a little like ballast.

Underneath the track bed 'shelf' I have planted Euonymous so that the railway appeared visually on top of a hedge. The Pecorama garden railway display at Bere in Devon uses a similar device to hide posts, which seldom find favour with 'the management', the partner who usually undertakes planting.

Gardens always seem to be rectangular or have corners where the railway curves round. The space behind the tracks becomes inaccessible if the track is above ground level. An easy solution is to plant an evergreen shrub that can be trimmed by leaning over the railway.

### I titled this book 'from the ground up' because we will spend quite some time on the ground!

Perhaps the most taxing of all our work is the laying of track onto the base that we have prepared, awkward on hands and knees – in Winter – in the rain.

**My basic track laying toolkit. Plastic Padding for instant fix to base, hold for about a minute here I use bricks. Track nailed to mortar base, or mastic adhesive to concrete. ( Nails hit stones in concrete). Pliers squeeze fishplates. Copper conducting grease filling makes electrical contact and allows expansion. Tenmille-G. track here.**

This is why some like the insulating block and direct screw method. Though I recently had success on a couple of 1000Metre layouts again with a two centimetre thick mortar bed and masonry nails through the sleepers. This method was timed at three minutes per join, five minutes per length.
Your locomotives may well manage tight curves but they will wear out their wheel flanges, and the track, and possibly their motor gears unseen. Never lay Flexi-track under tension. A mixture of flexible track, with a rail bender, and a few pre-bent curves purchased is probably best.

### Extra time taken to lay track as near perfectly as possible will protect expensive rolling stock as well as guarantee good running for whatever trains may run in the future.

Our track will be exposed to the elements at all seasons. The brass rails will expand and contract almost visibly, as the sun shines on them. The difference between frost and full Summer sun will be significant. There is no need to lay track with a fixed gap between lengths but a gap is needed. On a hot Summer's day in sunshine, no gap. One millimetre in Winter at fishplates will do. Two rails touching at low temperature will cause trouble later.

# Level Crossings action

*Every two weeks a car stalls on a level crossing, once a month someone is injured. I have written (many times) against building garden railways at ground level if at all possible. One of the main difficulties is arranging for tracks to cross a pathway or steps. There will be extra cleaning from muddy shoes treading directly on the line and worse – the danger that a train will cross just as a large foot occupies the same space has happened to me, and my new £1000 Elsa.*

**This railway runs around front and back gardens, This means that it must cross the garage driveway and paths.**

**LGB Alaskan White Pass diesel and Bachman Shay hauled lumber train passing.**

My very first railway was around a small garden and crossed three paths. I abandoned it quite quickly. For some of us, we do not have a choice, and the railway must be at the same level as the lawn, patio, deck, or pathway.

There are some working model level crossings, one, from LGB that opens with the weight of the train, but I here am talking human sized crossings and the ability to sense either the train or the human (or animal). A passive infra-red (PIR) or motion detector switch is usually found with outdoor floodlights. The idea, is to switch off the track current when someone nears the path crossing, and on again when they have passed.

Our old friends, LGB have produced grey plastic infils that clip between the rails of their 'standard' track. This means we can take the path right up to the outside level of the rails and have removable pieces between. This also makes tramways appear more realistic.A 'passive'alternative is to raise the path over the tracks as a humpbacked bridge. For crossing steps, run tracks under a step as a tunnel, not over. With higher level tracks, insert a removable bridge or lifting 'bar flap'.

## Track Cleaning - Leaves on Your Line?

*Adhesion was never a problem with steam locomotives. They had axle loadings of up to eighteen tons – nine tons on a wheel. Modern 'lightweight' diesel, and even lighter electric stock rely on willpower to stay on the rails. Leaves can disrupt traffic.*

During the filming for the television series we visited Bekonscot Model Village in Buckinghamshire and there we discussed track cleaning. Sadly it was too quickly dealt with in the programme later titled 'Buildings'. We should have expanded the topic, because we had trouble with digital control through the rails, possibly from bad contacts everywhere. The locomotives could pick up running power because of multiple contacts but the radio interference could have affected the wireless control of the digital system.

There is a very good heavy tin-plate 'maintenance' cleaning wagon from Marklin Gauge-1 at under £100 from Gaugemaster. This has two excellent long sprung abrasive pads, easily replaceable. (The couplings need changing to your preferred manufacturer). This wagon could be attached to any train, any time, for a daily cleaning top up. LGB supply similar wagon ' stick on' units too.

**Dick is a dab hand with a track cleaning pad attached to a broom handle, reaching into tunnels. – from our favourite retailer!**

I have seen the work of several commercially available units. One with grinding wheels that go backwards – they judder - and clean in patches (most people reverse the motor supply), an American offering with small rotating grinding wheels for each rail, and of course several that slowly push a heavy grinding block along the track.

Taking a four wheeled box wagon, cutting the underframe's centre portion and moving it along, I made room for my cut down rotating 'sanding disc'- a drill accessory from Black & Decker, with its replaceable extra fine 'wet & dry' sanding sheets. These are unlikely to grind the track away with repeated use, or disintegrate in the wet.

The major challenge was to find the right power for the disc. A secondhand 12 volt cordless drill motor and chuck. Batteries could also provide adhesion weight.

**The LGB track cleaning blocks are great for cleaning soldering irons too! LGB Capito has vinyl colour scheme and transfer logo.**

The LGB heavy L87403 metal wheels with pickups are ideal for such uses and cost under twenty pounds for two axles. Only one of these axles is really needed to pick up current for the motor – from the cleaned rails *after* the cleaning disc! Heavy wagons also need the roller bearings or they will suffer axle locator wear.

There are a few suppliers of model motors if spare loco motors are not available. The catalogue from Maplin Electronics (www.maplin.co.uk) not only has motors but gear sets, chain and sprocket drives and 'projects' for sound modules. There are others from MFA/Como Drills in Deal, Kent, an extensive range with and without gear boxes (www.comodrills.com) and listing voltage regulators. Good model

**Big yellow track cleaning loco with contra-rotating abrasive wheels used on this public display railway. Here switched to normal running. Pinoso Railway, Alicante, Spain. Opening 2006.**

shops that stock model boat parts and racing cars will also have drive shafts, boat propeller shafts, and 'universal couplings' which mean that the shafts can be out of alignment or have a small angle and still work – like a car's prop-shaft universal joint.

Model boats also have G-Scale searchlights and various detailing items that transfer to railways. The standard source for big model motorising and accessories is the Ripmax catalogue and handbook. This is a veritable bible intended for all other modellers *except* us big scale railway enthusiasts. The Handbook lists dozens of motors and gear sets for all modelling purposes – some will travel at a true 60mph and demand 50Amps! (The working aircraft landing gear looks ideal for motorising level crossing gates).

### *It helps to have a gearbox rather than 'direct' drive because this will change high rotational speed into high torque and lower speed.*

The Maplin worm set seemed to give the right rotational speed, with a COMO 918D 12-24Volt motor. The 'slack' in the cogs allowed the shaft/disc to move up and down for bad track joins. LGB 'Special Oil' 50019 quietened the gear 'chatter'. Because the rubber and metal sanding disc is quite heavy, gravity presses it onto the rails. It is important to get the shaft vertical for equal effect on both rails. I also fitted a Diode which will only let current pass one way to ensure the correct rotation direction for the disc, which would unscrew if allowed to rotate in reverse.

Lastly, and I'm always impatient to get to this stage, a raid on the 'spares' box provided a Bachman figure along with an LGB trackworker, and some plastic for the disc guards – we don't want any railway workers falling into the spinning disc.

Adhesives are always a problem. I moved some of the existing wagon detail and glued the doors shut.

For added safety because the front wheels are free to 'steer', I added some fishing weights over this axle. I removed the projecting front coupling but if the wagon were to have a tendency to derail, it could push a small (weighted) 'industrial' wagon from the LGB 'Field Railroad' series, or small weighted Bachman truck. This would act as a 'pony truck' for the wagon, guiding it round sharp curves, just as locomotive wheels do.

If the model were to be battery driven, then a sealed scooter battery or a YUASA 12Volt 2Amp- hour unit (Maplin) would be fitted. Either of these batteries would run the cleaner (and a pushing 'Stainz' loco) for a few hours, and be recharged on a normal car charger. Otherwise NiCad / LiOn rechargeables. If you follow the battery powered route, its adviseable to fit a 'tilt switch'. These use a blob of mercury (conducting liquid) that moves away and breaks contact if the wagon derails. They are used on windows in burglar alarm systems. (Maplin RN 22Y).

*With its new red paint job, topped off with some waterslide transfers (decals) from GRS, the operational track cleaning unit was ready for export to the San Miguel Railway in Spain. I was sure Laurence the Chief Mech E. there would be pleased.*

# 7. Electrics and Electronics

*Life in the 21ˢᵗ century demands a familiarity with electrical apparatus and for many a basic knowledge of electronics. The microprocessor is everywhere, from toasters to garden railways. This warrants a brief excursion into the realm of Volts, Amps and transistors.*

First, a word of warning – do not embark on any project unless you have a grasp of the principles involved. Do not tamper with the mains or mains powered devices, and always fit a sensitive circuit breaker between the house mains and the whole of

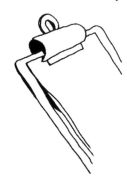

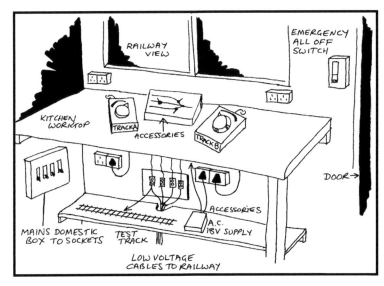

your outside railway supply. I also use a 'consumer box' with a breaker outlet to each mains device, the controllers, soldering iron, kettle, fixed in the workshop/shed, with a master cut-off switch at the door. Always get a certified electrician to check any mains wiring.

This electricity may be a simple 12 to 24 Volt D.C. supply but will need to be controlled to make the train perform much as the real thing. Accessories, such as points and signals may run on A.C. because this allows smaller powerful motors.

**'Jumbo' controllers above, 5Amp supplies from shelf below. Car battery chargers for 12volt lighting on floor. 'Knife' switches cut supply to isolated parking tracks overnight, the controls are never touched. Buffers have shuttle circuit boards inside.**

I provide a 'ring main' cable carrying A.C. from an 18volt transformer and join points or signals locally to it.

Shuttle units from LGB (in buffers) or Gaugemaster are sited on the shelf here, rather than outside – they don't like damp, some even go rusty.

Outdoor railway modellers have many options for their motive power source, including a supply of electricity to the rails for locomotives to pick up, or batteries carried on board – for power or for lighting.
We are usually confident in our approach to A.C. mains electricity and simple controllers that reduce this to a useful model current. However, the field of electronics is viewed with trepidation.

The easiest introduction that I can find to electronics is the use of a silicon diode. A small black blob, silver at one end, black at the other. A wire projects at each end.

### *This 'semiconductor' (almost a conductor) diode device lets our D.C. current flow one way only.*

Never again will your trains hit the buffers, even if operated by heavy handed friends. We simply cut the positive feed rail about a foot before the buffers and

**Basic toolkit: Pliers for fishplates, multimeter to test supply, and controller for track power if needed.**

**Lionel G-Scale Hudson loco passing.**

solder the diode across the gap. (the diode must be capable of handling say, 50V and 5amps. There are many sizes).
Now, when a loco approaches the buffers it will stop at the gap because no forward current is flowing. When the current is reversed the diode will let it flow across the gap to the loco which will back away from the buffers.
Usually the silver (or white) end is the way the current flows out of the diode. The cost? A few pence each. Every buffer should have one!

With growing confidence we could add a light-emitting diode which will glow red when the train arrives and is stopped. Especially useful if the buffers are out of sight and you have a (long) wire back to where you are with the red LED where you can see it. A basic form of train detection.

There are many more simple uses of modern semiconductors and circuits in our railway modelling, and many excellent books. Sadly very few deal with our special needs. We operate out of doors, in all weathers, and we use quite high currents compared to smaller scale modellers. Our trains may have four motors, each needing 24Volts at 1 amp or more, and we may have several carriages with lighting.

Here is another electronics topic for use to take into account. The lighting on our locos can be 'directional'. That is, the lights come on for the direction the loco travels. What is used? The diode we first encountered!

These will then switch the loco lights on according to the direction set on our controller.

Reverting to the track supply, reversing loops have always caused difficulties to railways with two-track electricity supply. When we construct the familiar single track 'dog-bone' we will have a loop at each end. When the train runs round the loop there will be a 'short' in the supply and the loco will stop.
However, we can fit a simply built circuit (LGB make one for digitals) and while the train is in the loop, change the controller direction, to watch it run round and out, back along the line it used to enter.

One of the most annoying features of model trains is their apparent inability to move off slowly then with gathering speed as in real life. We advance our controls while nothing happens until the train shoots forward. This requires built in 'inertia' to our system. Model locomotive makers have tried to overcome this with more 'poles' to their motors (LGB 7 pole Buhler) or a three pole rotating 'armature' in a massive permanent magnet ( a ring-field magnet).
Others have solved the problem however with a system called PWM (Pulse-width modulation) where the full power is fed to the loco but in pulses and it is the gap between that is varied until there is effectively no gap at full speed. Beware, this control system tends to heat up the motor – it is always running at full current – so ventilation is a factor. Secondly, the quick rise and fall of the current can make the motor 'buzz'.

We can also use capacitors to smooth out a current flow, perhaps from our controller. Specifically the charging up and discharging of the capacitor to slow down and stop or time certain operations for our trains (Gaugemaster and LGB). The LGB 'Jumbo' controller allows slow-down to be set using track reed-switches. This 'does everything' unit also allows the setting of a 'residual' 6.3 Volts track current, to power sound boards when locos/trams/wagons are stationary.

The 'first buy' simple device for the toolbox is a 'voltmeter' or 'multimeter'. When its two wires are connected by touching 'probes' to our two rails, the dial will tell us what the voltage is. We can see this drop when a train speeds up, and measure the drop from input point to the farthest part of our track. The meter dial measuring say, 25Volts can be fitted to a control panel and inscribed in 'Miles an Hour' so that we can assign 'speeds' to various parts of our tracks and also see what we must do to retain a given speed up hill. This makes our locomotive 'driving' more interactive and interesting. Useful pocket voltmeters cost under five pounds.

**Loco magnet operates reed switched accessories. The scored lines are from between rails debris and projecting fixings – screws, nails.**

Train detecting and equipment operation needs another small device, the *reed switch*. This small component, two wires in a glass bead about three centimetres long is a simple switch. However, it is operated by a magnet. When we place a magnet near the wires they will close, then spring open as the magnet moves away. See the connection ? If we can fit magnets to our locos, then as they pass over a reed switch fixed between the rails, something can be switched.

This system could operate signals, a whistle sound, or a level crossing

### These electronic aids can make our railway operation more like the real thing, and allow us to drive the locomotive and train with much more realism.

There are many ways of 'track bonding' so that electrical continuity is kept all over the layout. Permanent is to drill a small hole in the web of a rail and solder a wire (0.5-1mm) through it. Wire can be soldered to the two rail ends after laying. Seaside layouts invite corrosion. There are rail clamps (expensive) that are very good.

I use copper or graphite conducting grease and solder the wire (indoors), to a fishplate which is fixed tightly over the two rail ends. This lasts up to ten years.

**A can o' worms?**
**A weatherproof distribution panel trackside.**
**Wired with domestic mains cable to reduce loss, low voltage goes to track and accessories.**
**Yellow plastic isolating fishplates join the rails. Track feeds are soldered to brass fishplates.**

**Trains are running – and it's raining, but John knows what he's doing!**

The latest system is 'digital' control where the controller tells many separate decoders what to do. Visitors must also be fitted with decoders that do not have the same 'address' as your own locos!

Non module fitted locos will run on a digital supply. *(See Digital section)*

One of the more unusual aspects of big-scale train operation is the sound. We can fit sound generating electronic modules to our locos that will reproduce exactly the sounds from the real prototype locomotive.

These modules use track pick ups and loudspeakers hidden in the loco or rolling stock. Good Hi-Fi practice is to use as large a speaker as you can, bond it to a large surface, in a box, with holes to let the sound out fits the bill. This will amplify the sounds, and enhance the base frequencies.

### Sometimes we can use a reed switch in the track to operate a loco whistle fixed just inside a tunnel mouth.

Weatherproof (Mylar) speakers suit this purpose. A tape of your favourite station sounds could be relayed into a building. (or Boxcar Willie's wild west hobo music) Modern MP3 players can be used to record live railway sounds or download from the web to play back. I know they are meant to hold 20,000 heavy metal tracks for my daughter but we old 'uns can get with it too. There are locomotives that reproduce sounds, and their own station announcements, while they are stopped (batteries, or about 6.3 volts to the track).

A word here about signalling. The movement of our trains in the garden is one of the enhancements that a garden railway makes. The movement of signals adds realism. Not all of our signals have to move but it helps if some do. Except for those who model some European lines where coloured light signals have existed for many years, most signals are up and down (semaphore) arms. The most effective is to mount two or three arms on a gantry and have only one moving.

There are various coloured LED units that will glow red or yellow, quite brightly for use outdoors, if we wish to make working coloured light signals that simply light up appropriately. These can be fed from track voltage. An amber LED can be fitted next to the firebox doors and fed from the loco pick-ups to simulate the fire. *(The appropriate valve resistor will need to be fitted in series with the LED).*

**Low loss wire from signals and point motors is checked using test track and A.C. feed before installing outside. Wire will be hidden.**

**Paint pen identifies motors against track plan numbers.**

Just a little more about signals! When we stop a locomotive there is a long trail of rolling stock behind it. This means that the loco may be 'safe' in the siding or platform, but the last coach or wagon might still straddle the points? Some guard's vans have wheel pickups for lighting. Our trains can be fifteen feet long. Whatever we do, we need to be aware that the loco is not the whole train. GRS supply two types of signals, pole and lattice, in a wide variety of styles, working and non.

**Testing! Train approaching points is about to activate a reed track switch. Next time round it will stop, and activate alternate train on the second isolated track. Yellow plastic isolators. 13A Domestic mains cable for track feeds. Grey track feed to fishplate. Red to reed. Accessories a.c. ring main supplies point motor via reed.**

Not all railway modellers are wedded to narrow gauge live steam. There are some of us who liked the mixture of steam and diesel in the mid twentieth century. In the 21$^{st}$ century we can run inter-city expresses at quite high speeds around our railways, so providing express passenger and slow freight if we wish.

Mainline practice begins to creep into our operations. Our signals would not be complete if we did not have a 'theatre' indicator! This is a matrix of light bulbs in a square, 5 bulbs by 7, that lights to show 'F' or 'S' . Thus telling the driver which tracks he is about to use. Sometimes this may show the platform number assigned to the train or for a route – left or right diagonal (Maplin).

There are outdoor British mainline station models available now for the first time since the 1930's.

Perhaps easier than you imagine, burglar alarm miniature t.v. cameras allow us a driver's eye view of our railway for the first time. A colour camera for under a hundred pounds, comes with a receiver to plug into your television – involve the family!

# Digital - Control for the 21<sup>st</sup> century

*Until the end of the twentieth century model railways mostly used electricity for power. This is because of the ease and flexibility that it provided. There were and are very many gadgets available to provide low voltage variable supplies. The electric sewing machine has a twelve volt motor and a foot pedal accelerator like a car, press down to go fast. Trains historically have been controlled from a hand sized box with a large rotating knob on top, the custom with many domestic and industrial devices.*

Now that we have miniaturised music recording, telephones, and the computer is as available as the telephone, we have become accustomed to a digital world, where information is broken up into tiny fragments – digitised. The historical 'analogue' systems, where something increased to make something else increase as an analogue, are fast disappearing or gone. It is simpler to make everything 'digital'. Cutting down track wiring.

The latest innovation is to send coded information along with the track current. Each locomotive, even each accessory, can have a coded 'address' and our controller can send an instruction to only that address. Even more wonderful, a different instruction to each address, we now have individual control.

Consider the possibilities, we can 'double head' two locos on a train and combine their instructions, well, we could do that before , they had the same track voltage. Now, we run those two locos at different speeds, in different directions – at the same time, even on the same track. We can tell points to move – a different address. A recent LGB Henschel shunting loco ('switcher') has digital control uncoupling, on the move if desired. When friends come to see the new wonder, we can give them their own controller addressed to a train of their own, while we control our favourite.

***From here, there is a small step to operating the trains by computer, this is already a digital device.***

Locos must now be fitted with a 'decoder' sensitive to their particular 'address'. While these new locos will run on old analogue controlled tracks, old locos will not run on digitised power. Not all old locos can be retro-fitted with a decoder, so beware that bargain more than a year or two old.

Usually, our control of trains is by wandering hand held television style remote, a common 21st century device. This will communicate with a 'main station' box in the shed, fed by the mains. The box is connected directly to the track rails, can be wireless (R/C), and control locos as well as points.

# Digital Command Control
## LGB Lenz Multi-Train System

*Introduced in 1995 this digital system was designed in co-operation with Lenz Elektronik, a leader in command control. The plug-and–play simplicity even allows use of non-decoder equipped locos in old 'analogue' mode.*

Since 1995 LGB locos with a 'D' moulded on the gearbox are high capacity decoder (55021) equipped. LGB agents will not install decoders into 'Shell' gearbox (with a seam across the bottom) fitted locomotives. Small LGB locos require an (55022) decoder unit to be fitted by LGB agents.

The older track cleaning loco cannot be operated with the system, even using the 'analogue' setting. Loco motors running on 'analogue' may make a buzzing noise. Newer loco's can be fitted with Decoder's in most cases.

All powered rolling stock, including sound wagons will need a decoder. Acessories, such as points and signals need their own decoder (around £45) and address. Power is taken from the track (it's A.C.) and up to four LGB point motors can be hard wired to the box, which needs extra weatherproofing, perhaps in a lineside hut.

Massoth, who make the LGB branded system also market under their own name, a more robust and fully featured DCC system. There are several manufacturers entering the field.
Aristo-Craft Train Engineer 2000 has a PWC setting for Aristo locos, and 'linear' setting must be used for LGB or electric 'spikes' will damage the electronics.

Vienese Digitrax manufacturer, Zimo –'System 2001' has a function that overrides individual loco decoders to stop any train at a red signal, or station. The units supply 8amps and 16amps (with a booster unit) for larger garden layouts.
*The system can incorporate a large graphic display, or a computer screen with a track diagram*

Always consult your local stockist or a club to obtain advice for your requirements, before spending your hard earnt money. If you start off with the correct equipment for your needs you will save money in the long term.

# 8. Motive Power

*One of the hardest decisions to be made at the planning stage is the type of motive power. I hesitate to give advice on a very personal choice. This is often determined by the locomotive that we have just bought and is sitting on the mantlepiece. Following the premise that a large percentage of garden railways are built and run by those primarily interested in railways, the nearest thing to a real locomotive is a live steam powered model.*

The most common power has been track electricity supplied from a remote controller, in a shed, or wireless connection to that controller as a 'master' track feed. This is how the latest digital systems work, enabling control of a dozen trains and accessories all at once, from a wandering hand-held device (see digital section).

**This Aristo loco has the lowest running gear track clearance that I have seen with little room even for magnets underneath.**
**Note:**
**Couplings are not always at a 'standard' height from different manufacturers.**

Track power allows us to chose from many off the shelf products. We can also supply the same level of power from on board batteries, because we have plenty of room in box cars. When we need pulling power, we can use motor cycle lead acid sealed batteries. Recharged with a Halfords car unit, one of these will run a train all day, and give good adhesion too!

We only need to feed current into the tracks at one point. Usually in the shed near the transformer, or master controller. The best conductors are those heavy lumps of brass out there, the rails. We still need to feed power to signals and accessories, and we do this with heavy domestic 0.5mm twin and earth cable as a 'ring main'.

**Even with pantograph down, this LGB 'Capito' is among the tallest G-Scale locos. The snow plough at front sticks out sideways at tight curves.**
**Mallet cab comes close for height, also the wood burning chimney of a Stainz.**

By applying electricity to the rails, and so, all parts of the railway, we can control separate trains each with a different frequency radio receiver. This could be in a wagon. We can also welcome visitors with or without radio control this way.

The automotive industry is built on twelve volts (trucks on twenty four). There are many cheap and reliable gadgets and modules for motor cars that we might utilise.

Batteries and chargers, light bulbs, timer modules – from your car's interior lights?

With so many choices 'off the shelf' for our locomotives, a bunch of catalogues, or several magazines will be the best source of information. For those who wish to build or 'kit bash' the club or society will provide answers. Locos are available in r.t.r. (ready to run) form as well as kits, adaptable to 32mm or 45mm. Left, San Cheng handmade in brass for GRS, a GWR class 45xx 'Prairie'.

One of the greatest trials that we face is the sudden arrival of friends or family " to see the trains run". If we did decide on battery power, we can dispense with some of the rituals and avoid track bonding. Any live steamer will take tens of minutes to raise pressure in the boiler, most track supply layouts would need a rail clean. We cannot neglect this at any time, or there will be a build up on the wheels. Debris removal might be achieved with one of the snowploughs available. I use a wagon with rotating lavatory brush – a new one that is!

# Live Steam

*The whole subject of steam motive power requires a section on its own. There are exhaustive books on the subject. Those of us who wish to embark on real engine driving generally have a different kind of railway in mind. To place a live steamer on an electrified line will surprise us. There will be hills, unnoticed before, where we must open the throttle. The loco will run away if we do not pay attention.*

**GRS Elsa. My first and perhaps our best live steam loco. Damaged – line at ground level, the day I first ran it. Repaired, and we never had a problem.**

This is the real driving experience. The weight and friction of our 'consist' the train,

will affect our driving, and we must stop for more water, and fuel, oiling our engine while we fill up, possibly every half hour. Quite a lot of this engine oil ends up on the tracks, along with condensed steam. We also begin to understand the professionalism and skill of engine drivers and firemen. A whole new world.

We also get dirty. ( *again – see Last of The Summer Wine* ).

Live steam is truly an outdoor hobby. Lighting a fire and boiling a steaming kettle has serious safety implications. Locos become very hot and cannot be touched. We cannot walk away for a cup of tea and abandon our locomotive. A derailment indoors could be a disaster. Children must be supervised. But it is great fun.

The attraction of driving your own locomotive, different to any other, means that you must open and close the throttle in anticipation of the demands of the 'road' ahead, and your load. This is not the case with diesels, or our small scale electric traction. Sensitivity and knowledge are lost, driver/fireman teamwork has no place.

### *Steam loco 'drivers' will benefit from a 'steaming bay' for start-up and maintenance. This is best accomplished, I believe, with some track above ground level.*

Live steam at least starts off the ground. The tracks still have to be kept clean and free from oil and water. Boilers, usually made of copper, need to be pressure tested/certificated for sale or public running. With live steam comes responsibility.

Live steam is very well supported in all the garden scales, at all prices, and models integrate well with electric systems because they have insulated axles.

There is a surprisingly long list of live steamers available ready to run. Many more come as kits. Perhaps the best advice is to start simple. This also implies low cost. Models start at £150 and rise to thousands. The majority, and all of the most economical models are based on narrow gauge prototypes or are 'freelance' narrow gauge 'might have been'. Many are available as 'dual gauge' or in different gauges. Above, a real working narrow gauge loco cab at Launceston.

**Radio controlled live steam GRS 'Elsa'.
Batteries and receiver (Rx) in the tender.
Coaches from Playmobil.
Plywood track base on posts amongst foliage.
Teenagers are attracted by the technology.**

I believe that most of us start with electric traction and aspire to live steam later. I built my second railway with ten foot radius curves ready for main line live steam.

My first purchase was a GRS live steam radio controlled 'Elsa' The tender housed the radio gear. This lovely blue loco is still my all-time favourite. I built line three on a rockery in the corner with 2ft6ins curves just for this loco, and the teenage children. It ran beautifully there, and on my 500M main railway. Its pressure gauge was very helpful, the single flue and directly filled boiler (refrigerator ice, de-mineralised water or de-scale it every 6 months) raised steam in under 20minutes. I never 'boiled dry' but that's not too serious anyway.

A loco more basic than this started me on big-scale live steam. The Mamod company made several stationery steam powered engines – and a locomotive for 32 or 45mm gauge tracks. The modern derivative is about £150 using solid fuel tablets. Really a toy, it goes (and stops) and introduces many to the skills and excitement. PPS make 'Janet' with more improvements at under £400. Locobox offer 'Oliver' at under £500. These now have proper reversing levers where we can easily reach them. Roundhouse 'starter' loco 'Millie' has an externally fired gas boiler, non-insulated wheels, gauge 32 or 45 at around £400. Their 'Sammy' is internally fired at just under £500.

Going up the price ladder, and complexity, towards the £500 mark, we should see boiler pressure rise - from about 15pounds per square inch to an average 40p.s.i This enables locos to pull 12kilos or more. A lubricator will push engine oil where it is needed. The Accucraft live steam locos – 'Edrig' (£400) has insulated wheels, and fixed cylinders replacing oscillating types.
Please note that we still have not reached the price of the only 'OO' indoor live steam locos on the market – from Hornby in mail order catalogues at £500.

A loco that models a prototype and has the necessary radio control – otherwise you must run alongside to alter settings – will approach or exceed £1000. My 'Elsa' was such. Roundhouse 'Billie' is a lovely 0-4-0 much like the LGB 'Stainz' and with working (Walschaerts) valve gear at just over £1000. 'Joan' – prototype at Welshpool & Llanfair, 16mm scale, 32mm or 45mm gauge, internal gas fired, reversing lever in the cab, insulated wheels, very detailed, under £1000.

Models of prototypes off the shelf include some rare items too. The Darjeeling railway locos, ClassB 0-4-0WT in miniature Gauge-1, with water gauge, steam regulator, safety valve, pressure gauge, lubricator and gas regulator, 365mm long, radio controlled option - £1850.

**Gauge-3 GWR Prairie tank from GRS. Brass bodied electric or live steam, for about two thousand. Seen here with an autocoach**
*GRS*

Aster in Japan, started producing their live steam (and/or electric) models in the 1970's. Their slightly small Gauge-1 range ( 1:32 scale ) includes A3 'Flying Scotsman', A4 'Sir Nigel Gresley' or 'Mallard' and a GWR 'King', weighing over 7kilos, with full Walscaerts, four cylinders, displacement lubricator, axle driven water-feed pump. All ready to run or kit form. Using a small suction fan on the chimney until the loco's blower can take over, steam can be raised in a few minutes.

***These models are faithful reproductions and are priced in many thousands. Their secondhand value increases. We have to compete with investors for ownership.***

*GRS*

Sadly, no one has fitted a seven inch long whistle into a Gauge-1 0-4-0, you can't scale it down. The real chuff-chuff is also absent with model steam.

Aristocraft have overcome even this last difficulty for us. Next year, we are promised more new British outline 1/29th scale from Aristo and Accucraft, neither G-Scale or 1/32nd. They already have an excellent and competitively priced (1:29) live steam, radio controlled 2-8-2 USA Mikado (it's plastic?). They have added digital sounds for steam, whistle, bell.

The best of both worlds!

Savings. Buy secondhand from a reputable source, average savings up to £200 on locos that cost £1000 new, look for special offers.

*GRS*

# 9. Customising & developing character

*Railway companies each came into existence to serve a purpose. Usually commercial freight of some kind. The railways that we now see preserved have public pleasure as their reason for being. Very few are there because they provide a needed service.*

Our garden railway then, should have a 'story', a history helps too. The railway that we built for the television series was situated in Saffron Walden, Essex. The railway was described as serving the Saffron quarries and carrying the product to the local docks. The passengers were only carried at weekends on pleasure trips. The railway had fallen on hard times and so bought rolling stock from all sources.

**The docks on the Saffron Line. Saffron is exported from here by boat. The tide is out. Abandoned mine under rockery.**

This explained the mix of British, Swiss and American locomotives. The railway thus had a 'framework' upon which we could build, selecting the curves and gradients for a rambling narrow gauge single track line. We provided an old disused branch into a quarry and had to bridge over the excavation. The docks were constructed using my polystyrene 'sandwich' and pond liner. This was punctured by a small boy and a large piece of metal. Mark Found, the presenter and railway's owner had the bright idea "the tide is out" and so he made sandbanks where the liner had become visible and the story was served.

**The Saffron Line had a junction station, and a halt at the docks, complete with life rings and rescue dinghy on the platform.**

These ideas grew out of my normal practice of providing 'set pieces' joined by the railway. This allows us to concentrate our efforts and money in places that we and visitors will view the railway operation. The track in between can be enhanced by planting and or the odd bridge or tunnel.

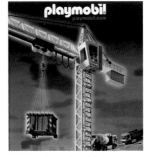

When all of this had been decided, and most of it constructed, Mark decided on a name for the line 'The Saffron Line', and a colour scheme – chocolate and cream. Some rolling stock was to be repainted and waterslide transfers used for the company crest on the carriages. The railway even owned a boat. This was an old coaster used to take the saffron to the main docks for export. In reality, the G-Scale sized boat I bought at a beachside bucket and spade shop on the Isle of Wight for £2.50p, repainted with figures added. A Playmobil dockside crane came from 'Toys R Us' and looked real from day one. All Playmobil is G-Scale and they have everything from police cars to red Indians, and pirates.

Railways began to take off at the end of the nineteenth century, and by 1900 were well established all over the major industrial areas of the world.

**Transfers, paint, or vinyl colours and logos give your railway an identity. Public displays have local business adverts which pay for rolling stock.**

*Locomotives were mostly supplied from Great Britain – still the crucible for live steam models today.*

The railways carried sugar in plantations, a railway in that bamboo patch?
Most railways saw the profits to be made from freight very early in their history. Carrying coal from mines – a rockery quarry? And to power stations, was more profitable than passenger traffic. Local produce – iron, mineral ores, farm produce such as milk, apples and livestock, was carried to major towns on freight trains.

Gold-rush mining in Alaska used the new railways. A mine tunnel and wagons full of gold? Few could afford it. When I visited, there were dozens of rusting abandoned locos at Sitka. Don't forget, the old GWR even flew aeroplanes – tri-

**It's not rocket science!
Radio controlled servo raises Estes rocket on arm. Contacts with loco power battery, fires and rises to 1500feet. Parachutes back – sometimes.**

motors, from Bristol. Have you got room for an airfield? Snetterton model shop sells great G-Scale Spitfires for well under £20, and ME109's - if you're with LGB!

Although we may be planning and building a garden railway, there is much that can be done indoors if we wish. The workshop is our Winter home. When we have created a name for our line, we can devise and order crest transfers for our trains, customise paint schemes.

Locomotives should be named. You can carry on the tradition, loco nameplates in brass (GRS) can be family names, or football clubs?

## Do You Have
## a Modern Image ?

*Starters in the hobby go for the dominant supplier with the broadest range and the reputation – LGB. They model (vaguely) G-Scale German and Swiss preserved narrow gauge for the biggest markets, they say, in Europe, and the USA. (A quarter of Americans are German, and the new young America voted narrowly to speak English, not German) LGB have some modern trains too, (out of scale), but not British. If we want British railways, with only a few (but increasing) G-Scale British models, we must chose Gauge-1, or gauge-3, or 16mm.*

However, there *is* a contemporary modern train from LGB. So modern that the original runs daily at 300km an hour. It also had the greatest ever German rail crash a few years ago, derailing its fourth coach and piling up against a bridge. LGB model this Inter City Express, their all-white LCE. There are two versions around because it was first introduced as a Lehman 'Toy Train' (discontinued) and now with a new front section shape, as LGB.

Similar trains to this appear in many colours throughout Europe, even Japan, and its shape is close enough to accept several British train company's liveries. There must be well over a dozen colour schemes running on British rails, from First, GNER, Virgin HST and their Pendolino to Channel Tunnelling Eurostar. In this model we have a truly up to date modern image. Who dares make that tunnel under a pond?

**LGB modern LCE starter train set can easily become a Virgin Trains HST or Pendolino. Brass nameplate – GRS.**

The train comes with a 1Amp controller and some track, in a giant 'train set box' at a bit over £150. The 'OO' equivalent is the same price – just for the train. There are extra carriages (a restaurant car) and motor bogie with train indicator lights. This model is in white, which makes for easy changes of paint finish. The train is large, and empty, and with just a few small Posidrive screws, easily dismantled. There are dummy pantographs that just pull off – a good idea because they tend to rise, and hit your tunnel portals. The transfers come off with a hair drier.

### *Don't throw the giant box in the dustbin – why advertise to everyone that you have a big railway?*

Using a 5Amp power supply and a long straight section, the motors give off an audible whine and the speed is quite realistically fast. I have used the LCE as a surprise element on a couple of public display railways now, and small children seem drawn to race alongside the train. I use a cheap (Argos £5) 48 segment timer to run the train every fifteen minutes for fifteen minutes. This cuts down motor wear and keeps the interest. The motors and gears need a little TLC every few weeks.

**GRS**

The only fault with the model is the transfers, particularly the windows, which fade to nothing after about a year in sunlight, (watch the one in the television series 'Bridges' programme). Not really 'drinnen und draussen? as printed on the box I have converted the LCE with two virgin colour schemes. The first was produced by spray painting, and this 'prototype' – for the Hobby Co. is in the LGB museum already I am told! The latest train was converted with self adhesive ultra thin vinyl sheet as used on commercial vehicles ( and hovercraft!)

I chose to paint the yellow warning patch in Humbrol 69 using Tamiya model masking tape – the best available. I also rubbed a dark grey paint lightly over the bogie detail with my finger and put yellow on the axle boxes to indicate roller bearings! There is a wealth of detailing wasted in the black plastic underframes and running gear.

**Gauge 3 wagon kit from GRS G-64 range.
White metal underframe and detailing.
Water slide transfers and coating solution.**

*(Yes, I painted it in the wrong livery.)*

Adding an extra coach (560mm long) needs an extra motor inside the 'empty' rear bogie. With anything but very sharp curves, two motors just manage four carriages total at 1 Amp plus. An LGB magnet fits into the *rear* motor bogie underside to switch points, but be careful if you use it to 'station stop' or 'park' the train. If you use an isolating section to stop the train, however long, and use the first motor to stop the train, the second, still on powered track three metres behind, will keep turning.

***With wheels spinning faster than Downing Street press office, you'll get some real 'rail burn'.***

Overall, this train is cheap and capable of great adaptation. Everyone likes the model's apparent speed. Family and friends have all travelled on a Virgin HST and recognise it immediately. *Below, my 'Western' diesel and battery power box car.*

In another leap forward, Aristocraft produce the first British outline loco in G-Scale by a major manufacturer. Not 'Flying Scotsman', but a class 66 diesel for around £300.

When you get tired of meandering narrow gauge historical slate quarry operations, get out on the main line and watch a heavy freight train, or an express flash past!

# Railways and mountains

*Many modellers chose unusual or obscure railways for their garden. The two most common of these variations are rack railways and overhead electrification catenary. In mountainous areas and whole countries, such as Switzerland, railway construction and operation presented exceptional difficulties. How did the engineer provide a railway up a slope of one in four – a 25% gradient?*

A quick and easy solution was to pull the trains with a rope and a steam winch, one car balancing another. These railways still exist in many tourist resorts around the world. *At left, Torquay, modelled at Babbacombe..*

For flexibility and power, however, a locomotive was the answer, but how to overcome the adhesion (the grip) problem. The answer seems simple enough, a cogwheel on the locomotive, and a toothed rail along the track.

***The engineering principles are quite straightforward, but the precision of the engaging cog and rack requires more care in track laying and maintenance.***

Thus far, only one manufacturer allows us to model rack railways in our gardens. The LGB range includes the basics needed to provide a rack railway on a steeply sloping hillside garden, or a rockery setting. There is a selection of locomotives and rolling stock. The all-important rack and accessories is simple to use and well thought through. Though the locomotives modelled are Swiss, very minor modification and transfer crests will turn them into Snowdon Mountain Railway, or that up Snaefel, Isle of Man.

**Gone to lunch?**

**No. The rack has to be inserted in its clips from one end, seen here snaking at right of track.**

Great care must be taken in laying the foundation for the railway, the track base (formation). For a concrete or constructed base 'formation', his should be reasonably 'levelled' without humps and dips. A long straight edge will serve.
The track bed itself, preferably flat mortar can then be laid on top of this and levelled to better tolerances for the rails.

The second of the two most important considerations is the 'transition' from level to slope or slope to level. Just as we are advised to provide shallower curves before the main curve left or right in our level tracks, so we need a shallow curve upward before the main upward slope of a rack railway. The transition from level to sloping track is also best achieved on the straight. This is to allow the centre cogwheel to engage properly in the rack.

Even more important, is to make the curve at the top of a hill, from slope to level, as large and shallow as possible. There is an obvious and common sense reason for this – so that long wheelbase rolling stock will not 'ground' on the rack or tracks as it passes over the 'hump'. Another problem is that couplings will come adrift, with the ever present danger of 'runaways' downhill to the bottom!
LGB recommend an extra hook fitted in couplings without one, and supply special rack couplings (grey) so that the usual uncoupler piece which projects downwards is missing. A vital point, various manufacturers have different heights for their couplings – beware!

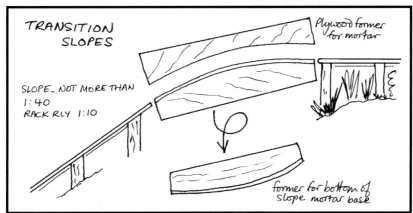

TRANSITION SLOPES

SLOPE – NOT MORE THAN 1:40
RACK RLY 1:10

Plywood former for mortar

former for bottom of slope mortar base

The rack system comprises a toothed extra rail fitted between the rails, using clips that grip the rails and hold the rack centrally, with its teeth projecting above rail level about 3mm. This provides a hazard and requires caution in an outdoor setting. Beware mower blades!

A wise precaution is to use four or more 'clips' per metre, and even more at curves, to keep the rack central. Longer rail lengths, with fewer joins are probably a good precaution too.

The rack height and projection means that rail cleaning becomes a problem. With a block, only one rail at a time can be cleaned.

For reliable and powerful operation, the rack locomotives may require more that the usual two amps. A wise move is to utilise a five amp supply to provide a margin for longer or heavier trains.

***Looking back to real railways, the greatest friction that a locomotive has to overcome is a sharp curve and an upward gradient. This also applies to our models.***

## Catenary

**…and it rained, all day. For television, the catenary railway – see the programme!**

Catenary – the shape made by a hanging length of wire. Some of the rack locomotives have overhead electricity supply, picked up by an extending pantograph. Included in LGB's catalogue there are also normal locomotives with rooftop pantographs that extend and 'collapse' depending on the direction of travel. This gives the European modeller opportunities to combine rack and level catenary railway operations.

LGB supply all that we need, including two heights for catenary suspension posts.

Catenary and rack operation requires the best possible setting for the railway, to minimise the potential pitfalls outdoors. The rack's top transition 'hump' presents clearance problems that must be considered. Using more suspension towers will keep the wire at a continuous height from the tracks. Some enthusiasts use 'OO' rails and fishplates for the overhead supply 'wire'.

**A small garden space filled with railways and their infrastructure. Even catenary - at top, rack at bottom.**

**This display railway at Weston-Super-Mare – mostly Pola and LGB**

Catenary operation brings its own problems – of cleaning, overhead pickup in tunnels, wildlife damage. However, the realism is enhanced when all works well.

Luckily, the locomotives all have track pickups and so a little cheating can allow us to run through tunnels and overcome some of the other difficulties.

Lastly a couple of pictures to tempt you to attempt your own customising. I know that it takes a little nerve to take a saw or knife to a detailed model, but it can be rewarding, and you have to learn sometime?

John started adapting his Playmobil at a young age. Here, he is completing work on the working snowplough conversion. Rotating a loo brush was the clever part. The motor came from my old Black and decker drill. (it wasn't that old, and I was using it). The yellow wagon changed to a green box car holds scooter battery which also supplies the KOF diesel (on the shelf behind) as motive power. This is an old LGB item that was battery powered, yellow and with a big lever switch on the side.

**Kit bashing and 'conversion' takes a little nerve at first. Only the Playmobil G-scale crane lorry remains untouched.**

The second photo shows my own attempt at 'modernised' American railroading. A 'USA Trains' G-1 Amtrak loco, previously silver and lacking detail has been raised in height to G-Scale size, and pulls a Monogram (1:18) kit NASCAR racer in bits, on a flat truck. The watchtower comes with lighting and smoke.

# 10. INFRASTRUCTURE -Buildings and Accessories

## A potted history of railways

*Big-scale outdoor 'Railway' modellers never fail to appreciate authentic detailing of their locomotives and rolling stock. Track gets less than the same attention, and the few buildings bear little resemblance to the real thing yet the necessary weatherproof models and detailing are readily available.*

Once railway travel began to be accepted as a useful means of transportation, of people and freight, the serious exploitation of its full potential began to be undertaken by the Victorians from 1825 to 1875. With a high point from 1845, to 1847 when investment crashed. However, 65 years after that initial decline, the railways grew from 2,148 to 21,000 miles of network.

The first passengers were wealthy, important people with their luggage, even staff. The access points for the railway, the stations, took the form of country manor houses, following the practice with many vicarages, that other major building in the local community alongside the church. Manor houses themselves were often in the Tudor, Georgian, and then current Victorian styles. The hub of the typical country station was the main platform building, its size in relation to its importance and the traffic. Most stations handled small parcels traffic from a platform office. Brunel devised 'standard' small stations. His 'roadside with Elizabethan motifs' and 'Italianate classical'.

**Detailing items around this B.O.B. building are cast in white metal and come from the GRS extensive accessories listings. G and G-1 people are Preiser.**

The construction materials were whatever the local vernacular provided. The earliest were wooden 'clapboard' – cheap and quick. Then, bricks in red and yellow, or stone in many colours from soft beige to Welsh dark slate and Devon red or granite grey. Many parts of the country are rich in flints. These materials were soon used for decorative effect, and railway links meant that all materials became available everywhere.

The builders were all craftsmen then. Construction might demand 'Flemish' or 'Old English' bond for the bricks, twisted and top heavy tall chimneys.

The two-storied house of the Stationmaster – an important local personage, was usually on or adjacent to the platform. This would be accompanied by row of cottages nearby for the (up to) dozen or so staff under his command. There would be a cottage for the 'Crossing Keeper'.

From the start of the railway boom, the business developed very rapidly over a fifty year period. At this time, horses still provided the country's motive power. So too with the railways' ancillary business – the delivery of freight and parcels.

**Before the smogs, smoke abatement, and central heating, I remember ordering my coal at the station yard office, for delivery by railway horse and cart.**

### *At many stations there would be stables.*

Those at Staines were demolished in the 1960's. Paddington stabled over a hundred horses housed on three floors in a massive building at Horseferry Road, later converted to railway offices (where I worked) in the 1950's.

To handle freight and parcels for deliveries, there would be a goods shed, and its administration offices, usually adjacent to the platform and with access across it. The horsedrawn, (and later motor) delivery vans gaining entry through a large doorway from the station approach. This building could be quite large and alternatively might be at a distance from the platform, out of the way of passenger traffic. Most freight was moved at night. At the start of the day, the early morning milk would be transferred to the waiting milk wagon train here. Warehouses and

**Railways are about people, passengers and staff. Preiser have an enormous range in all scales and showing many activities. This typical G3 grouping is a mixture of Gauge-1 and G staff.**

factories would proliferate near to the stations. The goods sheds were reduced in number to become 'Freight Hubs' then they disappeared altogether.

Do not forget that when a railway came into being, even at the turn of the century, places now part of main towns and cities were still country villages. Paddington was a wooded country valley. Bromley, in Kent, was a country station at the end of the line. The station first constructed on this line was quite typical; a two storey stationmaster's house with single storey extensions, accessed from the platform. The single stories housed – the porters' room, including the lamp room, first class and separate ladies waiting rooms, the booking hall (and pay office) with a storm porch or possibly a canopy giving access to the *staggered* platforms – this practice was widespread, so that passengers crossing the line would do so safely behind any departing train. Footbridges came much later.

Off the end of the platform, would be a signals hut with its 'ground frame'. Later this would be converted to a lamp room when the Railway Signal Co. built one of their 'standard' new Signal Boxes nearby.
The inevitable level crossing would be manned all day from the Crossing Keeper's hut, and his cottage would be nearby, and the railwaymens' cottages. Nearly the whole of Swindon, Reading, Doncaster, Crew, were built by the railway for railwaymen, their dwellings, even corner shops and public houses .

***As trains became heavier and longer, and journeys too, the larger tender locomotives would require a turntable at journeys end, and to replenish coal and water.***

Along the way where there might be a siding for a 'spare' loco. There would be an adjacent hut for the extra men now required on these duties. At Pilning, the end of the Severn Tunnel, a spare engine was kept in steam. After four minutes it would be sent in to push a 'stalled' train out.

**Gauge-1 live steam often has little infrastructure. This line has a main station and the vital turntable. Engines in steam get hot!**

As the vast network of railways grew and expanded, as many as one in five stations became a junction, changing from a halt or line end to a station with its own branch. Bromley changed from country end of line for commuters to a through junction to the south coast, and Europe.

(Trains were run straight onto the cross-channel ferry boats). This required upgrading of track and imposed load limits of up to eighteen tons per wheel for big locomotives. Expansion created island and 'bay' platforms needing footbridges or subways. An engine shed would appear, to 'stable' the branch line loco.

**Station nameboards, previously overwhelmed by advertising enamelled signs, now had to be prominent. This was required because more travellers could read!**

The painted white platform edge, repainted daily, was only allowed to extend a short way down the end slope, for after-dark safety. There was a great deal of 'company traffic'. The weighing equipment was regularly checked by a man with a van – it arrived on a flat wagon. Brooms, barrows, railway bicycles for the staff came by rail from the 'company stores'. Remember Lonnie Donnegan's 'Rock Island Line'?

Because passengers travelled on longer journeys there would be overnight stays. Eager not to lose another commercial opportunity the station approach would acquire a 'Station Hotel' Paddington, and St Pancras excelled. Later, with faster expresses, local station hotels were sold off to become public houses – 'The Railway Tavern'. Brunel invented the 'Terminus' 'train shed' (still there at Bristol Temple Meads) for Paddington's four platforms – now fourteen! The Hotel was built around and above this. His intention was to show little outside but have all the facilities inside the station. Yes, he invented Public Toilets too!

Local politics would play a very large part in the moneymaking railway developments. When Brunel was refused permission to run his 'new fangled and dirty' railway through Oxford, he built his major station at Didcot, and a huge stationmaster's house in stone at Steventon (where I lived for a time). Oxford was (and is) later served with a branch line!

**Many of us run diesels, how would these refuel? The engine shed behind still displays its wartime signs as an air raid shelter for railway staff. Both model kits from B.O.B.**

The need for control of the expanding timetables meant that the original 'ground frames' working the signals and points could not cope. From the 1870's these were replaced with the now familiar signal 'boxes' with a lever frame placed upstairs, and a 'locking room' downstairs. Most railway companies had individualistic designs using readily available components. Walls often had clapboard siding and casement or sash windows adapted from the station buildings (SER, LBSCR). Some Chief Civil Engineer's Departments enjoyed designing their own whimsical constructions. The most commonly found designs had large window frames across the front, though this view was obscured by the communication equipment and bells. The windows at either end gave the view up and down the lines.

From the 1880's signal boxes were mostly provided by contractors, almost from a catalogue. The most common in southern England were from Saxby & Farmer. Even in the 1880's these had the 'modern' appearance that we all cherish. This company also supplied the LNWR. Other boxes came from McKenzie & Holland –

who favoured bargeboards to finish off the roof ends. Companies marked their territories with distinctively different 'boundary posts'. During wartime many windows were bricked up. Later, lineside memorials to railwaymen were erected.

It is very easy to lose sight of the fact that the railways most of us hold in our memories, up to the 1960's and beyond, were constructed almost a hundred years previously. The buildings, signal boxes, were developed over time, and were not fixed.

### Brunel's broad gauge gave way to standard gauge but the stations were not demolished. This gave the spacious GWR 'footprint' that provides today's large station carparks

The roofs of many small buildings would be covered in corrugated asbestos. GWR 'pagoda' waiting shelters were corrugated tin.

Staff always found time for gardening. This might include runner beans up the lamp posts, platform flowerbeds spelling out the station name. An award for the best kept station proudly displayed among the blooms.

**Specifically for starters in 16mm or G-Scale, this complete narrow gauge halt of four items comes in one box**

Railways were the cutting edge technology for transport communication. Individual railways always had a commercial reason to come into existence – and had to turn a profit. Stations only came into being as hubs for railway based activities which included not only the carrying of freight and passengers. The GWR had aeroplanes at Lulsgate Aerodrome Bristol. Many of our main junctions started out as country branches for agricultural produce – strawberries in South Hampshire. Many took freight from the canals, a reason for more interconnecting 'hubs'. Later taking away all the canal freight, especially coal for power. Short narrow gauge lines that formed a spider's web and were gradually absorbed.

The fact that **all** railways had a purpose, and came into being to make money for investors should not escape modellers. Railway modelling tends to concern itself with the recent or remembered past when non-profitable lines were being closed as freight shifted to the motorways.

The stonemasons, bricklayers and joiners who built our railways were craftsmen, proud of their work. It makes me sad to see a model railway trying very hard to be ''quaint' – the Master Builders were better than that. Track was properly laid, ballast kept straight and tidy along the 'cess'.
Next time you find yourself at a station, one that is not newly 'modernised' look for the stationmaster's house, the old cottages, the goods shed, stable block. Turntable pit. They will all be there somewhere, often heavily disguised by now, some even as an outline under the tarmac of the station car park!

## Model Buildings, accessories, people and detailing

Since 1960's the garden railway modeller has been at the mercy of the major player in the field, LGB. Naturally, this company models German, Swiss and sometimes even French originals. The big market is in Europe, and the next biggest is the USA which has many mid European roots. The largest of the spin off markets in accessories is of course model buildings. These have followed European and historic US mid-western designs exclusively. Many modellers have had to construct their own buildings, and still do so. However, there is growing trade support in this important area.

**Sculptor and model maker, Valerie Pratt with some completed new models.
The B.O.B. range reflects British railway infrastructure with highly detailed buildings in weatherproof resin.**

**British Outline Buildings www.railsidemodels.co.uk** models came into being to fill the obvious need for scale models of the real world environment that existed from the 1860's through to the 1960's when railways played a crucial role in our nations commercial trading success and growth.

*The B.O.B. range of approaching seventy resin weatherproof kits covers just about all our outdoor scenic-scales infrastructure needs.*

B.O.B. buildings can be left outdoors once properly installed. They offer one of the only two footbridges available. They also produce the only 'train shed' covered terminus since the tin-plate version of Lyon in the 1930s, now worth £10,000 if you see one.

Pendlebury Buildings produce bespoke items to order.

For European buildings we must turn to Pola (sometimes with LGB logo) or the more economical Piko. Both have extensive offerings, and include American structures for that large market. Adhesives need to be carefully selected. Though I have left Pola models out all Winter, some cover them with wooden boxes. Their catalogues are worth acquiring.

Less detailed terracotta and concrete cast buildings are available – though not by mail order! Application of the 'ten foot rule' helps us here. Garden railways and infrastructure are usually viewed from this distance.

**The castle is no particular scale but looks right in this landscape at Merrivale.**
*(And below)*
**There are many waterproof items such as castles, even a parthenon greek temple in our scales – for fish tanks! Look around when you shop there for your gravel ballast.**

However, the railway is a very personal project, and many prefer, or need to make their own buildings. The universal plastic scratchbuilder parts come from Plastruct, with a comprehensive range of thin profile high impact white polystyrene sections, angle, tube, and rod. There are many preformed sheet plastic products. These give us roof, stone, brick, wood textures. Perhaps the largest list is offered by I&G Steam who import from "5 miles north of Niagra Falls" for us. (01745 369980). Their booklet includes windows, doors, and foam plastic sheet on which to build the cladding textures. This is the one if you need a castle! You may have to take buildings into the shed for Winter, and do maintenance each season.

*MMV*

Slaters produce many wheels and wheelsets in all gauges. These are in the GRS catalogue which lists many of their own products, including station accessories such as chocolate and weighing machines and fire buckets. They also have an extensive range of signal kits to dress up any railway.

When it comes to populating our railway with staff or passengers we come to the second largest expense after the tracks. Most small figures will cost about three or four pounds. A typical carriage needs about a dozen figures to achieve any effect, so a train of three coaches will need three dozen people.

*There is no point in running trains with no passengers and none waiting on the platform.*

Building display railways usually requires over a hundred figures, and the Caernarfon railway needed a couple of large flocks of (50) sheep – G-scale.

Each passenger carriage needs 14 figures, from Preiser. Also, Aristo, George.Turner (for barges), Bachman, Imp, Aristo, LGB. Perhaps the best detailed really British *characters*, in 16mm, come from 'Busybodies' at **www.robbennett.org** .

Yes, it goes out in the garden. This 16th century inn model has weatherproof signs and transfers.

Burrago diecast metal car models are 1:18 scale. 'Memory Lane' stock British vehicles. GRS have GWR 'Trojan' 3-wheeler lorry.

Phoenix Model Developments supply detailing kits for Bachman, including whitemetal figures in kit form. Carrs Modelling have low melt solder for these. Imp models figures are whitemetal castings and include trolleys and an ice cream cart. I'm so antique that I can actually remember these!

While most of us prefer LGB couplers for reliability, adding an extra hook to the end that comes without one, American 'knuckle' or 'buck-eye' couplings are correct for U.S. trains. Kadee have a comprehensive range of G-Scale automatic couplings and these knuckles are the only type to uncouple magnetically for remote operation. There is no standard height – be careful!

Probably the only roofed train shed model on the market since 1939. The Virgin 'Pendolino' goes unnoticed by Homer Simpson as it pulls into the B.O.B. terminus. Reed switch box in track activates points and joined working signals. The Calbourne railway runs automatically.

I have often used 'plastic grass' simply because I can cut it to shape and it is instant ground cover. I stick or (big) staple it down, or weight with rock. Busch produce very good plastic trees, for indoor dioramas, but much more 'controllable' at the lineside around stations and buildings. You *can* put 'OO' outside - I use big 'OO' trees as little bushes.

# 11. A garden railway planting List

*A note about possible planting, while you build, plant! Your garden will benefit from some 'softening' of the hard boundaries and this can be achieved by planting low at the front and higher at the back of the side beds.*

**Seen from the train, G-Scale. The only non-living thing here is the ploughed field which is coloured and ridged mortar. The hedges and trees are clipped weekly and the fine grass is 'mowed' with sharp shears. Babbacombe.**

If you buy more mature trees/shrubs (larger) they might be a little slower and more difficult to establish, but the effect is a bit more 'instant'. Just plant with care, a little fish blood and bone, handfull of grit in the hole, water, and stake low down.
*Fence climbers*, Hedera (Ivy) 'Buttercup' is yellow, Goldheart is varigated
Honeysuckle, well drained, humus rich soil – sun/light shade.
Trachelospermum (star jasmine)- a bit 'tender'(plant near the house)
Surprise is always beneficial in a garden, so too with a railway that disappears to reappear somewhere else, so a few taller shrubs in front of the tracks renews interest. *(Tall thin yew - Taxus bacata Fastigiata).* It doesn't work to have the

**The opposite of an eyesore. This railway could be said to enhance the garden with its movement and delicate planting**

whole railway totally visible as you enter.
SHRUBS- 'bus station evergreen planting' gives an all year round 'skeleton' that will not foul the tracks and points with needles, fruit or tiny leaves. Viburnum and

Forsythia, Escallonia, Euonymus are all good under raised wooden track boards on posts, as is privet. The Peco display railway at Seaton, Devon has privet bushes under the post and board base at about a metre high.
*More evergreen 'skeleton' shrubs,*
Danae (dense shade, spreading).
Cotoneaster, low, wall hugging, red berries, small leaves.
Mahonia, anywhere, big leaves. Up to four/five feet
Pittosporum, any where, cut to keep small or 3M. If your soil is acidic – Skimmia.

**These plants are replaced every year, and left in their pots. Weeding in between is the only job.**

When you have uninvited access possible at the rear of the garden and valuable brass tracks visible, try pyracantha, (up to 6 feet) – the spikes on this plant will deter anyone, and you get nice flowers and berries in red or yellow!
Berberis is very spiked, anti- burglar. Same goes for Hawthorn (Cretaegus) this grows up to a  small tree.

You may not think that you have local wildlife, but once the railway is there they will make their presence felt!

***The planting helps keep creatures like cats, dogs, from damaging the track bed. More important – judicious planting keeps out uninvited human visitors.***

**Camomile, once established, needs no attention other than removal from the ballasted track.
Ground cover that is small leafed and low is not easy to find.
Passing  train is one of my LGB Gauge-1  LCE conversions to a Pendolino.**

This list is not exhaustive. Look in the herbs and rockery plants area at your garden centre. Our biggest problem is groundcover. We want very small leaved plants that grow and spread quickly. Nature takes a different view and usually small is slow.

Beware that very small conifers, so called 'slow growing' can actually grow to massive proportions in the fullness of time and good soils! Some plants, such as small leaved Privet, can be pruned with scissors to look like scale trees.

Bonsai trees – for about ten pounds (B&Q) are usually G-Scale.

In a rockery railway situation, and elsewhere, it is possible just to insert the plant still in its pot into the ground or gravel or crevice. This will restrict its growth further. I have again included some larger shrubs with spikes – also used to deter uninvited nocturnal visitors.

ARENARIA BALEARICA
Corsican Sandwort. Very small leafed (see Corsican Mint- brushed smell). Miniature lawn

AUCUBA       (SPOTTED LAUREL) Protect from wind damage. Any soil fullsun/part shade. Females will fruit.

BUXUS (BOX)
Tough, most soils and sun/shade. Prune throughout year. (Vardar Valley – mound forming) Edging box (suffruticosa) maintain at 12" Can be trimmed into living scale trees.

CALLUNA  (heather)

Extremely frost hardy evergreen, thrives in very exposed positions. Soil acidic, gritty, low fertility
(multicolor) 4" tall 10" spread.
CEPHALOTAXUS          (PLUM YEW)
(Nana) low growing spreading widely with prostrate branches.
(prostrata) 24" tall four feet wide.cushion shaped dome.
CHAMAECYPARIS OBTUSA  and PSIFERA Nana Caespitosa, dwarf conifer
CHAMAECYTISUS          (BROOM)
(Purpurens)  Low growing deciduous reaching 18" with a broadly spreading habit. Lilac flowers early Summer. Cut back when finished for next years flowers.
Full sun, very well drained, such as rock garden. Seeds or cuttings. Will not transplant.
COTONEASTER
Congestus Nanus tiny leaves grows prostrate. Mound.
(Dammeri) fully prostrate. Full sun, mod fertile, well drained.
(horizontalis) 3ft high 9ft wide.
(perpusillus) more compact smaller leaves.
(pendulus) 3ft mound trailing branches, berries.

Gardeners are used to waiting. You plant this season for next, even for a few years in the future.
Eager to get the track down on the base, the tunnel is built, and this railway owner couldn't wait to plant over it!
The delivery of two dozen small conifers will line the trackside and form a backdrop to passing trains.
The mound in the background is heaped topsoil, another no–no, because it will gradually sink and disappear.
Note the tall thin 'Arizonica' at left, the 'Lonesome Pine' of cowboy songs.

DABOECIA  (HEATH) Permanent moist, acidic soils, sunny. Trim after flowering. Low and spreading. Suitable for rock, heather, wall gardens.
ELEAGNUS  (variegata) evergreen, shade, most soils and positions,
ERICA   (HEATH) (carnea) spreading under 12"(Springwood pink or white -) spreading full sun well drained acidic prune after flowers
FORSYTHIA  Full frost hardy, any soil, compost or fertiliser to encourage. Sunny. Needs a Winter well below freezing to flower! Medium shrub.
HYPERICUM   (ST JOHNS WORT) Smallest – full sun fertile, well drained.Water late Spring Summer. Prune in Winter.
JASMIUM PARKERI Fragrant miniature jasmine.
JUNIPERIS COMMUNIS Compressa  Column type miniature conifer
LAVANDULA  (LAVENDER)  Full sun, fertile, well drained. Dentata woodier for hedges, trim after flowers. Fairly frost hardy.
LIGUSTRUM  (PRIVET)  Sun/part shade/moist/well-drained soil. Can be trimmed into G-Scale trees.
LONICERA   (HONEYSUCKLE) Nitida Baggessens Gold  tiny yellow leaves dense bush. Withstands heavy trimming  Small bush.
MAHONIA   Aquifolium  Windbreaks. 6ft Sunny, well drained, fertile better in shade no pruning needed. spikes

MENTHA REQUIENII Corsican Mint, small leaved, fragrant when crushed (by train or hand!). Groundcover.

OSMANTHUS (fragrans) 10ft. rich well drained soil sheltered position, sun or part shade. Clip after flowers.

PELARGONIUMS (regal var) 24" high sprawling. Cut back after flowering to keep compact.

PHOTINIA Protect from strong winds sun or part shade, bright red new leaves, prune to promote bushiness 2m.

POTENTILLA ERIOCARPA Grey green miniature leaves, yellow miniature flowers.

PYRACANTHA. (FIRETHORN) Sunny, do not dry out. Fruits on 2$^{nd}$ year wood. 6ft Dense hedges and screens - big thorns.

RHODODENDRON RADICANS 3-6inches high!

SANTOLINA Groundcover. Sunny, well drained. Cut back old wood after flowers. Tidy up in autumn.

SCLERANTHUS BIFLORUS Grasslike groundcover.

SKIMMIA Shade or part shade. Moist. Well drained, humus rich. (Japonica) Bush

TSUGA CANADENSIS. Minuta. Ten years to 6inches conifer

VIBURNUM Frost hardy. Well drained any soil, sun/light shade. Trimmed heavily after flowers. Bush

VIOLA YAKUSIMANA Incredibly small white flowers. Needs moisture seeds well.

**A waiting room in 16mm scale. The scale foreground tree, is - a tree, a bonsai from B&Q at £10. This miniature Azalea even has tiny white flowers in Spring. The Glyn Valley Tramway building is from J.A.Replicas by B.O.B. models.**

The Natural History Museum has a website that will tell you what soil you have locally and what will grow where. See the next section.

*PUBLICATIONS;*
*John Constable -- Landscapes in Miniature*
*Hesayon - Tree and Shrub Expert, Alpine Expert.*
*Nursery* **www.hythe-alpines.co.uk**

# 12. The 21ˢᵗ Century Web trains

*60% of all households in the U.K. now own computers, children use them all the time at school, as well as being used to chatting to each other with 'text' on their mobile telephones. We are buying more and more with the click of a computer mouse. Our children are being trained to do even more this way.*

The statistics show that web sales are increasing all the time. Stories abound of how we can buy our railway equipment cheaper on the Net, even using favourable exchange rates. Often we find that USA equipment and rolling stock is the same number of pounds as in dollars. A loco at £300 here can be bought for $300 using a credit card for protection. With over 1.5 dollars to the pound and allowing for exchange commissions and shipping that's a saving. You can't easily get after sales service though!

My own website has about a thousand 'hits' a week, and had 1000 on the day that it opened. Regularly, there are 'hits' from South Africa, Moscow, and more from the USA than Europe (about double). My catalogue for the USA is mailed out on a CD - to play on computer of course.

As a consultant and builder of railways I am pleased to see that the **www.trainsandtrees.com** team there have won national recognition in the USA for their railway designs. Here Titchmarsh and Dimmock still give us timber decking and 'water features'.

### The Net has also provided a forum where we can meet with railway modellers from around the world.

USA hobby has bigger following and much more support than Europe and UK.
Internet activity is also much more lively and expanding.
70% of my site 'hits' are from N. America.

We can join local groups and Societies who publish the latest news on the web. **www.16mmngmodellers.org.uk** will be known to many, and The G-Scale Society is a must at **www.g-scale-society.co.uk** as they enter their sixteenth year, in the 21ˢᵗ century. One of the newest sites, and worth visiting, is the Gauge '3' Society at **www.gauge3.co.uk**. Slowly, they are all being added to the **www.ukmodelshops.co.uk** site, which aims to be a major resource for us all in the U.K. Recently www.**gscalemad.co.uk** have joined the U.K. scene.

The USA has perhaps the largest and most active numbers of big-scale railway modellers. Hartland Locomotive Works produces 'Wild West' G-Scale trains **www.h-l-w.com** is their site. Last year a dedicated website was opened to encourage newcomers to railway modelling **www.worldsgreatesthobby.com** is worth a visit. I wish that we had something similar here though at ukmodelshops listed above, Adrian does a very good job indeed.

Another interesting U.S. site, since 1995, with special offers, a chat room, how-to information, thousands of photos and articles, interactive areas is **www.largescaleonline.com** you need to register and will receive e-mails on developments weekly. You could win an Aristocraft Mikado!

Farther afield, **www.gaugeonegallery.com** Australia, is the main dealer there, and sent me a nice calendar. Alphalink radio control and sounds – also from from Australia is at **www.alphalink.com.au/~rcs/** and in Bayswater Australia, **www.rcs-rc.com** radio control systems.

Some of the Major retail outlets have interactive websites, or only sell on line
Most of our major hobby shops have on line sites and communication. The biggest players are all there, **www.grsuk.com** Garden Railway Specialists, the first - with years of expertise, and a supplier of its own manufactured models .
In Sussex, 'OO' established supplier, **www.gaugemaster.com** have Marklin stocks. LGB at **www.geocities.co/hobbybahn** and **www.glendalejunction.co.uk** in Cambridgeshire. Kittle Hobby, have some gauge 'O' buildings, at **www.kittlehobby.com** in Swansea. Others are appearing almost daily – Garden Railway Centres **www.gardenrailwaycentres.co.uk** and the shop RAILS at **www.railssheffield.co.uk**

**The internet is growing in its use for shopping. New products can be brought to the market immediately on websites.**

Manufacturers too, have their sites where you can browse and download information – **www.railsidemodels.co.uk** were the first and list their weatherproof British scenic scales model railway buildings. They also have a 'what's on the Drawing Board' area for proposed new models. Japanese Aster locos (U.K.) can be found at **www.asterhobbies.co.uk** where their excellent but expensive illustrated catalogue can be ordered.
**www.bachmann.co.uk** will be familiar to many. Perhaps we might persuade them via the web to make their BR 4MT 80061 in Gauge 3, or Gauge 1 now that they offer the U.S. 2-8-2 Mikado live steam with digital sounds in 1:29 scale.
**www.lgb.de** -the website has great sound, and must attract our attention as perhaps the longest player since its invention of LGB G-Scale. Using the web and the **www.lgb.co.uk** site, we might all ask for more U.K. models?

*Some magazines have been a little slow to grasp the importance of this new information highway in bringing them new readers.*

Many smaller specialist sites exist now, and the number is growing –
www.br-standard.co.uk/pandj is the site for P&J Models. Electrics and electronics can be found at Kent Panel Controls **www.kentpanelcontrols.co.uk** KGR at **www.kgrmodels.com** and Roundhouse locomotives – www.roundhouse-eng.com and for the five inch 'size really does count' modellers, Maxitrack locos and equipment www.maxitrack.co.uk is a Mecca. Some dealers sell only on the web, in Scotland, **www.gardentrains.co.uk** contacts Sandy for you, and he has sound on the site.

Our own Garden Rail magazine is at **www.atlanticpublishers.com** who have many relevant publications, including Narrow Gauge World and unusually, GardenRail Weathercall. Railway Modeller is on the Peco site **www.peco-uk.com** with Continental Modeller. British Railway Modelling – **www.brmodelling.com** and Silver Link books at **www.nostalgiacollection.co.uk** are specialist railway publishers. All of these yet to become interactive and web publishers. The major internet bookstore and largest in the world is **www.amazon.com** with many specialist titles for us.

There are many peripheral sites that can be found by the 'links' from all of those above and which may take us in many directions. Listing modelling tools, equipment and materials, is **www.pandurohobby.whd.net** and **www,ripmax.com** is a major supplier to big-scale model aircraft, boat, and racing car enthusiasts. Electronics and electrics supplier to modellers (and inventors) is **www.maplin.co.uk** the catalogue includes batteries, model electric motors, and gear assemblies.

I hope that the addresses will be useful to many, and encourage others to look at the web for what it is – the information superhighway that will enable us to pursue our global modelling hobby in the 21$^{st}$ century.

# Computers
## and Virtual Trains

*So, most of us have found the delights of shopping on the web by now.*
*Some years ago, I wanted a new wrought iron garden gate. I telephoned the details to a local number, put the telephone down and drove for ten minutes to the manufacturer. My gate, exactly to my own sizes and specification was standing outside. While we talked, he had tapped the details into his computer, and a (car welding) robot in his garage had made the item.*

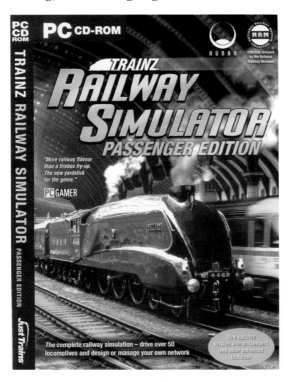

**Officially licensed by the National Railway Museum and developed by Auran, this claims to be the most complete simulation. Comes with a Driver's Manual too.**

When I last looked, Bill Gates, head of Microsoft, the world's dominating software company was down to his last forty three billion on his bank statement, so I am pleased that we can help him by considering his computer software specially for us. This is ***Microsoft Train Simulator***.

The idea is that you can run the programme and enjoy the golden age of steam as a passenger aboard the Flying Scotsman or Orient Express, even a Eurostar style high speed journey. The beauty of this software is that you can be the passenger, driver, or go outside and watch from various vantages as the trains swish past you through the countryside.

Once you have installed the main programme, you can go further with British railway operations. Starting with the *Engine Shed* add-on, you have ten loco types, from Iron Duke BR7 the V36 diesel electric and over twenty types of rolling stock too. *Euro Loco* add-on with TGV, Italian ETR500, German ICE2 also includes our own HST 125 however.

The 'simulator' goes further with *Train Sim Roundhouse*. This programme, which also only runs in *Microsoft Train Simulator*, includes Eurostar, Royal Scots Grey and Gordon Highlander, tank and ballast wagon trains.

Two more items expand the virtual railway system. We can go back in time with *Train Sim Activity Pack*. This allows over thirty 'missions' by train in wartime Europe,

**The software includes the exciting Carlisle mail train travelling through a serious thunderstorm in 1939!**

Lastly, well we always look at the instructions last, there is the book. The only official guide to *Microsoft Train Simulator*, with over 300 pages of advice, not only about the software itself, but about all aspects of railway operations, to assist our understanding.

There is also a re-issue of another software 'game' offering. *Trainz* now includes British trains. This software allows you to lay track, add the stations, buildings, bridges, tunnels. Then add the trains and passengers, even noises. You have 35 locos (including diesels) and about 50 types of rolling stock from 12 countries. The programme allows you to observe or drive.

The most widely known piece of software was made for the largest sector of the railway modelling hobby by Hornby. This was the *Hornby Virtual Railway 2002* (in a new 'special edition' from **www.eDREAM.co.uk**   tel: 0870 74 47 400)
Filling 2 CD-Roms this still costs less than £20 and includes twice as many locomotives from the Hornby catalogue as the 'standard' edition. You can update with a link to Hornby's website. After selecting your 'baseboard' size, and your 'room' there are 6 ready to run layouts and you can adapt these by 'drag and drop' with accessories making your own railways. There are even sounds for points moving.

While we are looking at the railways in a computer world, there is a growing array of relevant material for us. The most obvious subject for a 'simulator' is driver training. The *Locomotive Simulation* programme is based on the Settle to Carlisle section. This requires you to stoke up the fire for steam pressure, and operate meticulously detailed controls while the gauges display your locos status. There is a training sequence, and sound with synchronised movements as the scenery passes. This is an excellent way to learn about footplate working practices.
If its diesel you must have, the *Trainz* programme has cab controls.

Steam Railway magazine has published a  *UK Steam Railway Directory.* This is a detailed guide to 200 railways and 3000 locomotives. There are over 800 photographs for your enjoyment and modelling interest and a powerful search facility.

*Trains Galore* is simply a catalogue of 2000 railway images, all at high resolution detail so that they can be printed to illuminate our modelling.

All these software packages run on the ubiquitous Windows and some need a 3D card in your machine.

The main player in the 'built environment' field is of course The National Monuments Record which carries actual photographs of almost all of England's 360,000 listed buildings. These include many station buildings. The footbridge, signal box at Brading on the Isle of Wight Railway are there. The photographs are accompanied by the listing's detailed description. The address of their website is **www.imagesofengland.org.uk**

### Of course, there are many, many 'design your garden' computer packages. Soon, with a railway?

From **www.designyourowngarden.co.uk** where someone works with you on design and planting, to off-the-shelf garden design programmes.

There is a plant database showing what will grow in your area detailed by postcode. **fff.nhm.ac.uk/fff** is run by the Natural History Museum.

The railway modelling world is attracting the computer software writers because of the growing size of the market, and it is so pleasing to see that we can utilise the 21st century information highways to inform our outdoor modelling hobby

**Last word.**
**It may be the 21st century and we have digital everything, but the excitement is still the model train in a natural setting – outdoors.**

# 13. Join the Club

*my motivation for producing this book is not self aggrandisement, nor was the television series. My aim and hope is to encourage as many people as possible to join us, to gain more enjoyment from their gardens, to develop new interests in horticulture and to stimulate youngsters into a new hobby that can be 'hi-tech' if they so wish. Most of all, the whole family can become involved, and then become involved with others through the local clubs and societies social events.*

**There are clubs and railway preservation societies that major on one railway, now preserved or long vanished.**

The most obvious potential membership is the G-Scale Society, founded in 1987 and now with 20 area groups. The information exchange is supported by G-Scale Journal and also publishes a 'Technical Manual' for builders and operators of garden railways. There is an annual exhibition – 'G Rail'. Try www.g-scale-society.co.uk for full information.

For those who mostly favour British outline, and (1:30) 'fine-scale' live steam, is GIMRA, Gauge-1 Model Railway Association. This is the oldest large-scale and garden railway association in the world, offering a wealth of experience in construction and operation. There is a quarterly newsletter. www.gaugeone.org

With a smaller membership is the Gauge-3 Society whose models run on 21/2inch. Standard gauge 64mm track. G-Scale modelers are growing in numbers.

*The main clubs/societies in our garden railway hobby are mostly centred on each of the scales, or steam and non-steam.*

**GIMRA exhibit at the annual Ware show. Held in a garden centre where East Herts Model Engineering Soc. Have a 7 ¼ inch extended railway. 'Locolines' pullman coach.**

**The Association of 16mm Narrow Gauge Modellers**

Engineers might join The Southern Federation of Model Engineering Societies. Which has beneficial insurance contacts.

# 14. Public railway displays

*Disneyworld calls this Imagineering on a big scale, and I have devoted some space to it. The reason, building just a few big railway displays provides the equivalent knowledge of years of garden railway development when a modeler installs single railway in his garden, and it's what I do.*

There are about ninety public viewing railways in the U.K. and others in Europe. In the U.K. there are probably about 5000 private big-scale railways. Many host club meetings annually or for regular 'get togethers', Ours is a small number compared with Europe and the U.S.A.

I hope to set out here some of the most important considerations when designing or developing a model railway that will be publicly viewed for entertainment because there are lessons here for us all. A day out with a difference?

Imagine your garden and railway after 40 years. Babbacombe in Devon replaces all the buildings from a second set, and most of the planting every season. The 2 ¾ inch railway at centre has run two million miles.

Let modern museums be our yardstick. They are interactive, informative, and entertaining. They are the comparison by which a satisfying visit to a model railway will be judged. There is more common ground, because there will usually be a 'trail' to follow, by choice or in-built. Along this trail will be found the 'set pieces', congregating areas for viewing (lay-bys), and of course, surprises.

With a railway on the ground it is also often possible to see the whole layout at once, and any surprise or discovery potential is lost as soon as visitors approach.

This leads to my own rule number one, broken by me only with very good reason. – NOT at ground level. For many reasons. The most important are- wildlife attack, frost heave, viewpoint. Badgers will eat red electric cables (worms to them) and signals (ask a badger why). Heavy rains will undermine surface foundations and moles will see any cables and wires buried in the earth as their favourite foods, worms or roots. I am told this goes against the trend, let me know in five years.

**Pets such as dogs or cats (and foxes) may run around the railway, barging into constructions.**

Ground level means always kneeling down for construction or maintenance, and photo opportunities – scale 'eye level' is at about 6cms. Ground level also gives little opportunity for bridges or makes more work for interesting constructions such as ponds, hills, rockeries – the real railway engineering feats are found when obstacles need to be overcome by tunneling or bridging. A railway needs to be reasonably level but the terrain never is – except in deserts.

**Just look at those 'trees'.**

**One of the best gardens with trains is at Babbacombe in Torquay.**

The best height for simple viewing is about knee height, and for us more mature individuals who do not want to spend time in Winter and Spring on our knees, when we make repairs. If the closest set piece is at about half a metre high , then a garden seat gives a comfortable trackside eye-level view.

There is a second consideration, no paths over the tracks. This leads to all kinds of problems with level crossings and public safety as well as visitors throwing stones, cans, sandwiches, other children, all at or onto the display. Water is a great attraction for object throwing. Open railings do not really meet good safety practice, and walls create barriers that break the model world atmosphere. Paths also mean long tunnels underneath with attendant difficulties for cleaning and maintenance.

I mentioned seating. There should be seating at points of model activity or 'set pieces'. This gives the operator absolute control of viewpoint for maximum effect. It also gives a rest when viewing a large layout. A roof or gazebo will provide rain shelter (for us) while trains still run.

The question of display height and track plan needs careful planning. When there are several separate lines (a good idea), then the base track at around a metre with a top track another metre above, gives childrens' and adults' eye levels. This almost necessitates trestle bridges, viaducts, tunnels where lines might cross and disappear in front of us. Perhaps a rack or cable car to the top of a mountain terminating at eye level for children on dad's shoulders.

Changes to a railway layout are inevitable, not least for those who return. Museums change regularly, sometimes more than annually, and also have 'special' days. This may dictate some unused spaces and flexibility in construction. A robust track bed that can be walked on for maintenance but not six inches of reinforced concrete that forbids route changes. You will no doubt have bright ideas later and a new product could give rise to additional modeled activities .

I said before that museums today are, and have to be, interactive. There is nothing more interactive or interesting, or skill developing, than driving a live steam locomotive.

### All children play at being engine or tram/bus drivers. Almost none at being quantity surveyors?

Fortunately we now have some computer simulations from software producers –

even Hornby and Microsoft. A simpler way is to allow visitors into the 'control centre' for the railway and to make this as 'Christmas tree' as possible, all flashing lights and bells while being extremely simple, reliable and robust. A hands-on area – 'drive your own train' is easy to achieve with a simple and separate track for the purpose. Wandering radio control is simple in the 21$^{st}$ century.

Push-pull electronic modules are widely available, and 'station-stop' time delay modules. One of these controlling a train by push button is the most simple way of allowing the public to run their own train. Perhaps with automatic signals at beginning and end. Signs saying 'do not touch' when visitors can clearly see activity or interesting things is a no-no.

A public display railway, for adults and children, needs to contain accessible 'themes'. All railways need a theme (and a name) whether carrying passengers from A to B or coal and ore to the docks.

The Discovery Channel G-Scale railway in Saffron Walden, Essex, had it's story, was called the 'Saffron Line' with a saffron quarry and ore trains carrying the produce to the docks for shipment. There was even an abandoned mine and tracks – a 'set piece' area. 'Weekend passengers' traveled to see the mining operations - boarded their trains at Walden junction Station, with a halt overlooking the docks area. A model 'population' is vital. Sadly this railway owner's son punctured the dock pond liner and the docks area was quickly changed to a 'tide is out' scene!

Customising rolling stock with local businesses paying to have their names on wagons as simple advertising, perhaps even purchasing a whole train, offers a way to help with costs. There is a railway *in* a Macdonalds customised this way, and British Outline Buildings advertise their model kits on some public railways with customised advertising box wagons.

Typical current and almost essential 'themes' are Thomas the Tank Engine, recently available in G-Scale from Lionel in the U.S.A., Bob the Builder, likewise Noddy in Toytown. There are the Simpsons and of course Starwars – these figures are widely available in G-Scale, and I have used Luke Skywalker, and some Coronation Street figures waiting for trains on several layouts. Recently adding the Plasticine Pair - Wallace and Grommet – that famous train window cleaning duo.

The more traditional, zoo, farms, airfield, quarry, and trains carrying milk, coal, timber (hauled by a logging Shay), are all well received by the public.

Some or all of the above will have distinct and recognisable sounds, and sound is another essential. However this needs to be used sparingly and for effect. The trains will almost all come with high quality digital sounds nowadays. Some even have station announcements when they stop. A whistle unit just inside a tunnel, triggered by the train is simple to fit. A church with music, or bells from a weatherproof loudspeaker inside, *(there is one at Hidden Valley, Cornwall)* ships at the docks. Recently, sounds of farm animals have been included in wagons.

These masterpieces of the modellers skill, perhaps your own too, should not be handled too often if they are to last for public viewing, where everything must be at its best every time it is operated. A train can be worth a thousand pounds. This means that storage, and it needs to be secure, is a necessity. Insurance will also insist – along with 'public liability' at about a million pounds is usual!

Trains need to be stored at night or hidden for effect. Tunnels are a good hiding place, but not secure.

**Oops -Sorry, I'm in the way. A secure shed workshop and control centre. Lined with ¾ inch ply and insulated. Ply shutters for windows. Night store lines enter at left behind me. 'Spare' train storage on shelves.**

*A simple garden shed (on the outside) can be made vandal and burglar proof with thick ply on the inside and motion detectors.*

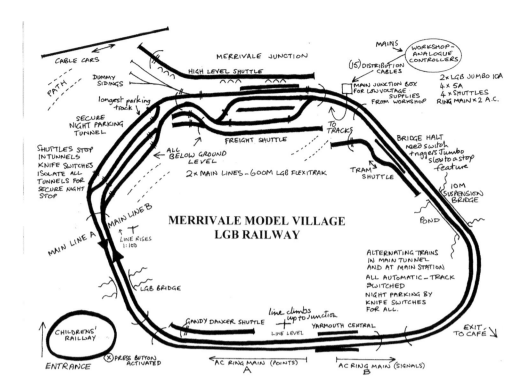

MERRIVALE MODEL VILLAGE
LGB RAILWAY

Inside, simply several sidings, knee height, to park trains. A CCTV camera here, with screen viewed elsewhere, will deter burglars but provide public interest as well during operations. Simple, cheap CCTV units (Tuxcraft) can be fitted on a wagon in front of a train for a driver's eye view.

Excitement and surprise can be helped by having an express or unusual train that runs infrequently, say , every twenty minutes, just once. Perhaps the Zoo train with animal sounds? The Orient Express?

To ease wear and tear and make the running gear last longer (a book in itself) two identical trains can be run. On alternate days, or one stops in a tunnel and the other emerges. No one will know and wear is halved, life doubled.

Additional interest for public railways is to offer local railway groups or even real preserved railway buffs, a venue to run their trains, on an 'open day'. This can be weekly, monthly or annually. Provision of a separate track is essential. Perhaps this is the above mentioned 'show train' track, round the outside which will be more accessible for breakdowns, which are likely, and will not really interfere with your programme for those who pay to see a display. It is not wise to hand the railway over on these days or there will be long periods when something does not run and visitors will expect to see the advertised display in any case.

**Groundworks started at Calbourne. Seen from the entrance. Sadly, the water filled trench around the layout was completed first!**
**The wall in foreground will have a rockery in front. Trains will disappear into a 'fake' tunnel behind.**
**The visitors line will run at left, from the shed/ workshop.**

The visiting railwaymen will need a 'railing point' for their rolling stock, and possibly a 'steaming area' for live steam locos (not at ground level please) this should have weather protection. All the trains can and will run in all weathers, not so the owners! There might also be tea brewing facilities.

Damage, and vandal behaviour are a fact of our life today. This causes a dilemma for the railway designer. The display needs to be visible but not reachable. A railway on the ground is the most vulnerable.

A railway in Florida has a railway 'Guard' in uniform, with whistle, to control the unruly and give information. Do not have stones handy. Tree bark around plants is non-throwable but may blow over the tracks. The opportunities for missiles must be minimised in the design. Trains can disappear into a tunnel where the public are very near, but features or activity pieces cannot be more than three to five metres away or the detail and operation is lost, so to the effect.

Allow for maximum expected numbers to view in comfort and stay for a half hour.

### A display in about a ten metre square can accommodate 25 to 50 viewers around the outside.

Make 'lay-bys' at viewing or photography points with dry paths in between (not gravel) and allow for wheelchairs and prams. The paths could go up and down, rather than the railway, to vary the viewing angles.

**Workshop and control centre at Merrivale. There must be enough room to store all trains over the Winter. The orange triangle is a 'rerailer' for trains.**

**The LGBtram has excellent street sounds see it in the new King Kong movie.**

Signage and information points are important. Firstly in controlling visitors, 'This Way Round' is the obvious directive. Public interest in how the display works, or was constructed, where the trains come from, their purpose, and ethos of the railway, are all important. Childrens' interest will be very different from adults'. Girls have a fleeting curiosity for figures and real-estate, boys - an abiding interest in mechanics. There are many who will be interested in the special planting for the railway – usually miniature leafed herbs and Alpines. Mothers and grandmothers frequently ask planting questions. A leaflet or other handy information is welcomed. This all very relevant to our domestic garden railway situations.

The educational value of a model railway display is equal to its entertainment and reflects the real world in many ways. After all, we are trying to create the atmosphere of the real world with our railway model. Railways were part of the industrial revolution, and continue to be the arteries of our commerce though second to roads and perhaps air transport. They replaced the horse as motive power, and the canals. Steam gave way to diesel, supposedly until clean electric traction would be the norm for the twenty first century. Speeds increased from 30mph to over 200kms an hour. The work of the railways, in transporting freight, and the engineering they employed with innovations and inventions along the way, is part of our history and also the development of technology.

It will pay to get the details correct. To build a railway display with an educationally valid theme it would be wise to involve local schools and or colleges. There are many projects of value to them, modeling for craft skills, electronics, mechanical constructions, even the design of posters. There are programmes available for wholly computer operated railways, though usually these are meant for indoors and not outside in the 'real' world.

**The railway base at Caernarfon.
This railway was built on a new heap of clay spoil and its long term stability could be a serious problem.**

**Even small gardens can benefit from renting a 'mini-digger' for a day. Mechanical help is always welcome.**

There are many ways to make the railway entertaining and informative. By construction of the 'set pieces', activity areas, interactive exhibits, surprises. Whatever is used must be simple, rugged, reliable, easy to use and maintain, and probably not expensive.
A trip to Disney World would not go amiss either!

The oldest of the public displays is probably the one at Beaconsfield in Buckinghamshire. 'Bekonscot Model Village' and its Gauge-1 railway, running among 1/12th scale buildings now with a newly built seven and a quarter inch gauge Maxitrack ride-on railway has been running for over seventy years. The full-size signal box operates eight trains at once. There is a coalmine, tramway, cablecars. For more detail try www.bekonscot.com .
Nearby is the long established Garden Railway Specialists shop at Princes Risborough, an Aladin's cave of big-scale garden railways.

There are other railways, and other model villages, perhaps the ancestors of our hobby. Bekonscot is beginning a museum on the topic and like Merrivale Model Village in Gt. Yarmouth, and Babbacombe in Devon, has items from the now closed Ramsgate Model Village. Most belong to the International Association of Miniature Parks. www.miniatureparks.org

# Railway modeling with a JCB

*If there is one place, more than any other, where you can find a whole raft of narrow gauge railways it's the 'little trains of North Wales'.*
*Imagine my delight as a railway designer/builder at being asked via the LGB importers Hobby Co. to construct a public display garden railway at Caernarfon, in the shadow of Snowdon. Especially since it might also be the largest in the U.K. (My design for Snetterton halted when they hit an underground stream).*

The designated area in the nature park was a heap of clay spoil about three meters high and 30M x 25M. On top of this was added a miniature 'Snowdon' about three meters to the top - six meters above the underlying ground level. I was a little concerned about stability and settlement of the new clay spoil heaped onto grass.
I had climbed Snowdon (properly) years ago, and been to Garden Rail's Welshpool Llanfair annual show of course, not far away if you visit.

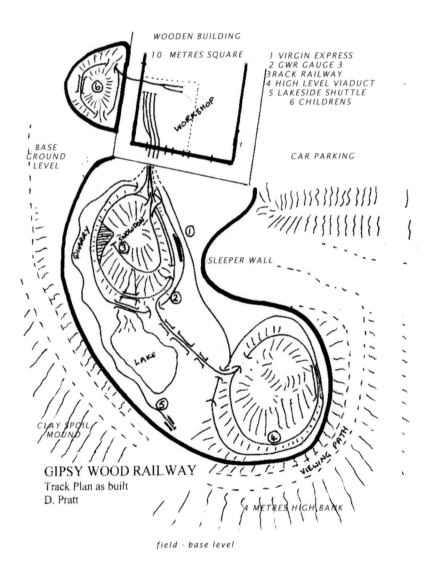

WOODEN BUILDING
10 METRES SQUARE

1 VIRGIN EXPRESS
2 GWR GAUGE 3
3 RACK RAILWAY
4 HIGH LEVEL VIADUCT
5 LAKESIDE SHUTTLE
6 CHILDRENS

WORKSHOP

BASE GROUND LEVEL

CAR PARKING

SLEEPER WALL

CLAY SPOIL MOUND

LAKE

VIEWING PATH

GIPSY WOOD RAILWAY
Track Plan as built
D. Pratt

4 METRES HIGH BANK

field - base level

Garden railways take many years to mature, but display owners need a show as fast as can be made. Bekonscot, Gt Yarmouth and Babbacombe are 40 years old and look just right as model worlds – in a garden.

Detailed plans were discussed and finalised. John Evans, the owner had already bought some equipment via e-Bay on the internet. His wife was planning The Gipsy Wood Park where all the animals are miniatures, and there was room for a model railway. It follows naturally that it should pay homage to the many local preserved railways – Talyllyn with double Fairlies, Welshpool, which runs LGB style carriages, north Welsh Highland Railway with Beyer-Garratt locos, even the local Great Orme tramway is worth a nod with several G-Scale tram models available.

Any display had to incorporate the Snowdon rack railway, and the LGB Ballenberg and powerful (long motored) Brunig HG3/3 locos look enough like those that might be found at Llanberis station, (across the road is the little Bala Lake Railway). So, the plan had included a three meter high pile of rocks – Snowdon.

### *This railway's landscape base was built using a JCB and a ten tonne crawler - digger!*

Many people arrive in the locality via a Virgin HST. For some time I have been converting the LGB LCE train as a high speed main line added interest. The only non LGB component of this railway is a Gauge-3 G-Scale GWR Prairie tank and Auto coaches from GRS, a reminder of the standard gauge lines via Llangollen, Corwen, and into Aberystwith. The wider Gauge –3 track emphasising the winding narrow gauge G-Scale tracks. The buildings are British Outline Buildings and Pola.

A logical topic for modeling is of course the main industry of the area, slate quarrying. Now only undertaken at Bethesda with explosives (LGB have made two explosives and exploding wagons!), but the employment life blood of the area for a hundred years and more. Vernon, working with me, had been a quarryman, ("slate splits better when its wet") so who better than to provide Vernon's quarry, where little quarry trains might be seen.

To add realism to the scene, the Pola buildings were selected from the catalogue when they could be effectively 'Anglicised'. The Quarry gained from this treatment with wooden and corrugated buildings.

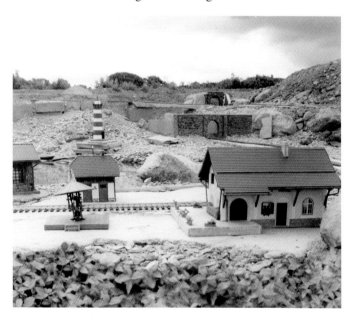

**Levelled mortar track base extends for buildings - on Welsh slate chips, available locally. Pola ABS plastic buildings are positioned for mastic fixing.**
**GRS concrete tunnel portals.**
**Trackside planting keeps pace with track laying.**
**Planted at foreground is a slope to keep public at good viewing distance.**

A standard feature of all my public railways is visitor interaction and an area for younger children – start'em young, before they get hooked on '00'indoors! I find that a big red button with 'PLEASE PRESS' does the trick, and an LGB starter set - with sound - keeps them interested. My daughter, a childrens' nurse provides vital information and searches out small figures of Bob the Builder, Noddy, the Tweenies, and any other current favourites, often from Halfords, or KFC freebies.

After two weeks non-stop intensive installation work, the railway was handed over when every train had completed its action three times before the owners, and ready for the planting to begin in earnest. The herbs and rock plants of three garden centres would be totally absorbed in the 30 x 40Metre railway area. The North Wales weather can be quite extreme with a minimum steady force 2 from the West. Mature trees will need to form a windbreak and each wagon or carriage will have to carry 500gms or more of lead (fishing weights or four inch nails) underneath or inside. The Snowdon railway is especially exposed. I use 'Stone Plaster' poured into coal hopper wagons and tankers, and the equivalent of half a brick in guards vans or end wagon of trains. This is because they have to guide any train reversing into the secure night store and workshop area. All rolling stock has coupling hooks fitted to both ends and metal wheels replace the supplied cheap plastic. The downward projecting uncoupler bits are cut off too, for safety.

Railway operations are as simple as I could make them with all trailing points, sprung so that trains run out onto their tracks but when reversed come back to the workshop start point. This also keeps the electrics simple and logical.

### The point's springs are from ball pens, adjusted so that the wheels will push them over without derailment.

All workshop parking tracks have diodes fitted at train length so that locos stop automatically for overnight parking when they enter, but run out freely.

I believe that with some judicious painting and the necessary carriage-side crest transfers (from GRS) the trains can give a good impression of local lines. A 'Double Stainz' representing a Double Fairlie acquired from e-Bay turned out to be a GRS adaptation made fifteen years ago and still running nicely, operating a shuttle round the 'lake'. They now have an excellent off the shelf model. They also supply an easy adaptor kit to convert LGB to a GWR guards van.

A purchase still listed for later is the LGB Beyer-Garrett, now selling at over its catalogue price when second hand (around £2,500) but essential for the NWHR which has several in various colours, runs from Caernarfon to Porthmadog, and can be heard running close by. Local outrage ensued when a driver was shot (with an airgun) while we worked. North Wales is wild country!

We earned a double page spread in the local papers, gaining a bout of curiosity visiting and I hope spreading the word about our outdoor hobby.

If you visit the Welshpool Garden Rail show this year – make a detour! You could also stay at the Black Boy Inn, modeled by British Outline buildings and displayed on the railway, near their Gresford station model (prototype once sited near Wrexham/Wrecsam).

*The railway is to be found at Gipsy Wood Park, 100yds along the Llanberis road at Bontnewydd, on the A487 about two miles out of Caernarfon on the road to Porthmadog.*

**The childrens' corner at Calbourne. An LGB Stainz with sound starter set circles a rockery, activated by a big green push button, which switches on an isolated parking section. This was operational within a few days of starting and is a favourite. The main railway layout is in background.**

*Just a footnote, the model village and railway at Polperro was being advertised at the end of the 2005 season at £650,000. If you're not already retired?*

# 15. Spreading The Word

*Once you've been on the box, and appeared in Curry's shop window, celebrity beckons. I've been recognised in the street, twice - " the fat guy with Mark Found".*

Positive Productions director David Hatter, and Tim his co-producer rekindled my previous career as co-ordinator at Bournemouth in the photography, film & television department. They spent early 2002 filming a fifteen part series on garden railways that has had numerous repeats on Discovery Channel.

*Available now on DVD from Video 125 (01344 628565) for under thirty pounds.*

The programmes were designed to whet the appetite of the general public, millions of them, as it turned out, every week for fifteen weeks. As a weekly show, this was as popular as any other, yet was in a subject that gardening programmes and magazines almost never touched. They prefer water features and timber decks, to the fully integrated and active scale model railway, with its special miniature and Alpine planting. Even the railway model magazines have neglected this growing hobby sector till recently. Now some have supplements annually.

The many experts consulted on screen, including my wife for her British Outline Buildings models *(Valerie wore a wig, at Bekonscot!)*, Bob Simes ex Tomorrow's World, passed on much personal experience and general expertise. Called 'series consultant', I began to think of the 'book of the film', including the areas that could not be included in a popular prime time television production where a large percentage switch off or on at each commercial break, but this never came to fruition. I hope that this book now expands some of those topics.

We certainly started something. In 2005, Hornby '00' (?) sponsored a Garden railway supplement by one of the model railway magazines, and I heard that Peco could be producing a DVD on the subject. Mark is promising a 'Railway Channel' on the internet and Garden Railway Rescue programmes.

There is much that can inform our outdoor railway interests, apart from the small but growing garden railway based information on the internet, and ignored by printed media. A study of aspects of real railway practice - in old photographs, books or magazines, television and DVDs is always beneficial to us. I worked as a ganger on the Watercress Line to improve my knowledge of steam and general practice – ending up as their bear mascot 'Watercress Willie'!

The main regular producers of videos and lately DVD's on our subject have been the chaps at GRS with MITV, owners of the t.v. catenary layout. Old friend Graham Whistler (Productions) produces some of the best on railway subjects. I bought his G-Scale layout when he changed to 5inch ride-on steam from Maxitrak. If he hasn't been to Darjeeling yet, he has plans to do some filming there.

# 16. The last word....

*We've been on quite a journey together. I hope that I have inspired you to consider, even embark, on a new and exciting hobby outdoors.*

*For gardeners, my wish was/is to influence you to look at miniature plants, Alpines, and of course, adding a railway to your existing landscape.*

*I have one request, that you include others in your pastime. I know that the garden railway hobby has something for everyone.*

When I worked in the Chief Civil Engineer's office at Paddington, I had no idea that forty years later I would be modelling those trains and lineside features around me. I rode on the last train through Bala, Corwen, Llangollen, and watched 92000 Evening Star roll out at Swindon works, I even pushed Caerphilly Castle into the Science Museum, now running again - modelled by Aster in Gauge-1 live steam. Helped dismantle Brunel's Chepstow bridge. I spent time in Rochester New York in 1965 and walked on the red carpet at Grand Central station. Now I run Alco FA-1 diesels with the exact same sounds I heard then.

But, I also run Eurostar and Pendolino – on 45mm tracks.

I know much more about miniature landscapes, Bonsai trees, and camomile lawns.

With my wife, we have learnt skills that we never dreamt would be ours when we 'retired'. Our range of model buildings, sculpted in clay, moulded in silicone rubber, and hand cast in polyester resin has made a whole new career for us both, and of course, designing and building railways for other people, which provided all the pictures in this book.

### Oh, and I am working on the next one already!

*They say you can't take it with you. This is the old railway at Merrivale Model Village. Angle iron tracks on bits of wood for sleepers. The track and the trains, like the buildings were all hand made. There were no manufacturers and local shops with our outdoor model railway equipment on their shelves forty years ago when four brothers built four model villages with handmade railways.*

**I just don't have a snappy caption for this.**

**One man's rubbish is another man's railway?**

**Suggestions on a (saucy?) postcard.**